W9-DBM-995

Contemporary Controversies and the American Racial Divide

Contemporary Controversies and the American Racial Divide

Robert C. Smith and Richard Seltzer

ROWMAN & LITTLEFIELD PUBLISHERS, INC.
Lanham • Boulder • New York • Oxford

ROWMAN & LITTLEFIELD PUBLISHERS, INC.

Published in the United States of America
by Rowman & Littlefield Publishers, Inc.
4720 Boston Way, Lanham, Maryland 20706
http://www.rowmanlittlefield.com

12 Hid's Copse Road
Cumnor Hill, Oxford OX2 9JJ, England

British Library Cataloguing in Publication Information Available

Library of Congress Cataloging-in-Publication Data

Smith, Robert Charles, 1947–
    Contemporary controversies and the American racial divide / Robert C. Smith and
Richard Seltzer.
      p. cm.
    Includes bibliographical references and index.
    ISBN 0-7425-0024-1 (cloth : alk. paper) — ISBN 0-7425-0025-X (pbk. : alk. paper)
     1. United States—Race relations. 2. United States—Race relations—Public opinion. 3.
United States—Foreign relations—Public opinion. 4. United States—Politics and
government—1989—Public opinion. 5. Afro-American leadership—Public opinion. 6.
Conspiracies—United States—Public opinion. 7. Afro-Americans—Attitudes. 8.
Whites—United States—Attitudes. 9. Public opinion—United States. I. Seltzer, Richard,
Ph.D. II. Title.

E185.615.S5815   2000
305.8'00973—dc21   00-020754

Printed in the United States of America

♾™ The paper used in this publication meets the minimum requirements of American National
Standard for Information Sciences—Permanence of Paper for Printed Library Materials, ANSI/
NISO Z39.48—1992.

To
Scottie, Blanch, Jessica, Scottus-Charles
Grace, Michael, Mathew

There are only three great national political issues:
bread and butter; war and peace; and black and white.

—Theodore H. White

Contents

Tables

Preface

In the days immediately following the acquittal of O. J. Simpson by a largely black jury on charges of murdering his former wife and a young man, one of the authors of this book (Smith) had numerous interviews with the media as reporters sought explanations, background, and context for the racial differences in attitudes toward the verdict. (In the October 4–6, 1995, *Washington Post* poll, 91% of blacks agreed with the verdict, compared with 39% of whites, a difference of 52%.) Invariably, Smith would attempt to explain to the reporters that this kind of division by color was not unusual in the United States; that the Simpson case was perhaps the most sensationalized incident of this phenomenon but that Americans were divided by color on a host of matters; and that a sensationalized murder case involving a black celebrity athlete accused of killing his white wife was one of the less significant instances of the racial gaps, gulfs, and chasms in American public opinion.[1]

Invariably, however, Smith's attempt to place racial differences about the Simpson case in the larger dynamic context of a society divided by color was ignored by the press in its single-minded attempt to make the Simpson case sui generis, something entirely new and extraordinary in the annals of black–white relations in the United States.[2]

THE AMERICAN RACIAL DIVIDE

Smith cited many examples of racial differences in opinion as large as (or larger than) that of the Simpson case, and more important in terms of the relations between the races and the capacity of the United States to endure as a viable, multiracial society in the twenty-first century. The examples included differences in ideology, partisanship, presidential preferences, policy preferences, and preferences even in television programs.

In terms of racial differences in ideology, one group of scholars locate 85% of black Americans (compared to less than a third of whites) in the most liberal opinion categories (a chasm of 52), while less than 7% of blacks gave responses that put them in any conservative opinion category (Nie, Verba, and Petrocik, 1976: 252–53). Writing of this chasm, Nie, Verba, and Petrocik concluded that such a uniform pattern of response as observed among blacks on measures of ideology is "an unusual phenomenon in survey data" (1976: 254).

With respect to partisanship, more than 80% of blacks identify with or lean toward the Democratic Party, compared with about 40% of whites, a chasm of 40. And not since 1964 have blacks and whites in majorities voted for the same presidential candidate; and even in 1964 there was a racial gulf of 35 (94% or more of blacks voted for Lyndon Johnson, compared to 59% of whites). During the 1970s, 1980s, and 1990s, the black vote has averaged 88% for the Democratic candidate compared to a 43% average among whites, a racial chasm of 45.

Similar gaps, gulfs, and chasms between the races exist on a wide range of public policy issues: the welfare state, affirmative action, national health insurance, and a government guarantee of employment. For example, on a composite index measuring six policy issues dealing with race, 63% of blacks were in the most left categories, compared to 9% of whites, whereas only 2% of blacks were in the most right categories, compared to 36% of whites (Kinder and Sanders, 1996: 27)—a chasm of 54 and a gulf of 34, respectively.

Less important but nevertheless revealing about the different worlds inhabited by black Americans and white Americans are their preferences in television programs. One might think that television as a mass medium would be a force for bridging the racial chasm, but no. Of the top-ten television programs in 1995, only one program, NFL *Monday Night Football*, bridged the racial chasm (Carmen, 1996). *Seinfeld*, for example, was number 2 among whites, 89 among blacks; *Friends* was number 3 among whites, 111 among blacks. By contrast, *New York Undercover* was number 1 among blacks, 122 among whites, and *Living Single* was number 2 among blacks, 124 among whites (Carmen, 1996).[3]

These chasms in television preferences might be viewed as trivial in an otherwise racially cohesive society except that the choice of television programs is emblematic of deeper societal cleavages. Preferences for *Seinfeld* rather than for *In Living Color* are not of much interest or consequence except perhaps to Hollywood producers and Madison Avenue. Preferences for mayor of Los Angeles, however, do have consequences.

In the 1997 Los Angeles mayoral election between incumbent Richard Riordan and former Vietnam antiwar activist and California State Senator Tom Hayden, the races were as divided in their choices of mayor as they are in their choices of television fare. In an election for which only 24% of the voters turned out, every discrete ethnic group in the city (whites, Jews, Hispanics, and Asian Americans) gave Riordan more than 50% of their vote, except, that is, for African Americans, who gave Riordan only 19% of their vote.[4]

Most of the studies of opinion differences, whether in the Simpson case or in politics and policy, tend to focus on blacks and whites, ignoring the increasingly multiethnic, multicultural character of late-twentieth-century American society. The results of the 1997 Los Angeles mayoral election suggest or at least hint that divisions in American society may be more than merely black and white—African Americans may be "exceptional" (Sears, Citrin, and Van Laar, 1995) in that they differ not only from whites but also from other Americans, including Asian Americans and Latinos.[5] In the Los Angeles mayoral election, 71% of whites voted for Riordan, yielding a black–white chasm of 52, but there is also a chasm of 40 between blacks and Asian Americans and Latinos.

The purpose of the foregoing discussion of the gaps, gulfs, and chasms between blacks and whites on a whole range of issues is to make the point Smith attempted to make to the press in the immediate aftermath of the verdict in the Simpson criminal murder case: The racial chasm in opinion manifested in the Simpson case is neither new nor extraordinary; rather, such divisions are endemic to contemporary American society. Thus, the inspiration for this book was to place the Simpson controversy in the larger context of post–civil rights era research on race opinion in the United States.

In addition to the Simpson case, we examine several other cases and controversies that have divided America across the color line in recent years. These include the Tawana Brawley case in New York City; the arrest, trial, conviction, and reelection of District of Columbia Mayor Marion Barry; attitudes toward Nation of Islam Minister Louis Farrakhan and U.S. Army General Colin Powell; opinions on the Rodney King verdict and the subsequent Los Angeles riots; and opinions on Supreme Court Justice Clarence Thomas in the context of the sexual harassment allegations of Anita Hill. We also examine racial differences in opinions on the Persian Gulf War. Finally, we look at "conspiracism," the tendency—especially pronounced among African Americans—to believe in assorted conspiracy theories.

RECENT BOOKS ON AMERICA'S RACIAL DIVIDE

As discussed in detail in chapter 1, there is a fairly extensive post–civil rights era literature on black–white opinion differences. We review this literature in chapter 1 as part of establishing a framework and context for analysis of the Simpson case and the other controversies. However, to continue Smith's point to the press during the first Simpson verdict, a perusal of several recent books on race opinion reveals that the notion that the racial differences in reaction to the Simpson verdict were sui generis would come as a surprise to scholars of race opinion in the United States, who see gaps, gulfs, and chasms in opinion between the races as an abiding feature, a structural characteristic of the nation.

Sigelman and Welch, for example, in their 1991 study, *Black Americans' Views of Racial Equality: The Dream Deferred*, wrote of "gross black–white perceptual differences" in opinion on discrimination (59); that "blacks and whites inhabit two different perceptual worlds" (65); of "a vast gap" between the races (107); of "an enormous perceptual gap" (78); and that "our dominant theme [is] that attitudinally black and white Americans occupy separate but overlapping worlds" (182).

Michael Dawson in *Behind the Mule: Race and Class in African American Politics* (1994) also wrote of "enormous gaps" in opinion between the races (182); of "deep and profound political divisions" (182); of a "vast political gulf" and of the "puzzling persistence" of African American political unity in politics and public opinion, despite increasing class differentiation (6, 48).

Donald Kinder and Lynn Sanders in *Divided by Color: Racial Politics and Democratic Ideas* (1996) wrote, "The differences are enormous, quite unlike any other social cleavage, and cannot be explained by black–white differences in income or educational attainment or indeed anything else. The racial divide in political aspirations and demands is really racial" (9). They also wrote that on many matters blacks and whites seem to live in "different worlds"; that the differences between the races on some issues are "simply staggering" (19); of how "emphatically black and white Americans disagree" (33); of a "huge and evidently persistent racial divide" (33); and "of the now familiar huge racial gap" (34). And Kinder and Sanders said that "differences as drastic as these simply have no counterpart in studies of public opinion" (27).

And to take one last example from the recent race–opinion literature, in *Facing Up to the American Dream: Race, Class, and the Soul of the Nation*, Jennifer Hochschild described the racial divide in opinion as a "paradox" that revolves around the fact that "blacks and whites live in the same society, have experienced the same history, are affected by the same political and economic events, and yet see the world in sharply and increasingly different ways" (1995: 8).[6]

Our major purpose therefore in this study is to place the Simpson and other controversies across the color line in the context of the race-opinion literature and the broader sociocultural and political relations between the races. We also will pursue the sources of these divisions beyond mere black and white, probing for race differences in terms of gender, social class, and age. In addition, although our focus is on divisions across the color line, we also pay attention to commonalities in opinion across the color line and to their sources. Finally, in the last chapter, we point to some possible bases for bridging America's racial divide or for dealing in a realistic way with those divisions that cannot be bridged.

PLAN OF THE BOOK

In chapter 1 we review the literature on race opinion in the United States, focusing on the fairly extensive post–civil rights era research. We discuss alternative theories or interpretative frameworks for explaining racial differences in opinion. We explain the data and the methods of analysis, the choice of controversies, and the selection and the use of the scores of surveys and polls that we employ. Also in this chapter, we include an analysis of the separate historical, social, economic, cultural, and political worlds inhabited by blacks and whites in the United States. These different worlds or realities provide a structural basis from which to understand black–white opinion differences.

Chapter 2 examines opinion differences between the races in general or on a broad range of race- and non-race-specific issues. This is useful in order to place the findings from the specific cases and controversies in the broad context of race differences in public opinion. In this chapter we use the National Opinion Research Center's General Social Survey (NORC-GSS), the most widely used academic survey of public opinion. The wide scope of the questions asked—ranging from issues of leisure and family life to those of religion and politics—makes the NORC-GSS an excellent resource for this purpose. Also, its large sample size of 3,000 allows us to conduct detailed intraracial analysis of black respondents as well as white respondents.

Chapter 3 looks at racial differences in opinion on U.S. foreign policy in general and then at two recent foreign policy controversies: (1) a detailed study of the Persian Gulf War and how it divided the country by color and (2) a brief account of opinion differences on U.S. policy toward Haiti.

Chapter 4 examines how blacks and whites view prominent African American leadership personalities, including Nation of Islam leader Louis Farrakhan, General Colin Powell, and Supreme Court Justice Clarence Thomas.

Chapter 5 deals with various conspiracy theories—some directly relevant to the black experience and others dealing with broader questions of trust in the government's willingness to honestly and fairly deal with the American people. Opinion here among both blacks and whites is profoundly cynical and alienated, expressing a strong tendency toward conspiracism. To provide some context and perspective, we also look in this chapter at racial differences in attitudes toward the paranormal as a prism through which to view the broader issue of belief in conspiracies.

Chapter 6 deals with four cases of crime and punishment: Tawana Brawley's allegation in 1978 that she was assaulted and raped by a gang of white men in New York City; the 1991 videotaped beating of Rodney King by several Los Angeles police officers and the riots that followed their acquittal; the arrest, trial, conviction, jailing, and reelection of Mayor Marion Barry; and, of course, the O. J. Simpson case.

In chapter 7 we summarize our results, place them in the context of the literature on post–civil rights era race opinion, and discuss the implications, both theoretical and practical, of our work for understanding and dealing with an American society divided by color.

We would like to thank the Office of the Vice President for Academic Affairs at Howard University for the university-sponsored Faculty Research Award, which defrayed the cost of acquisition of the numerous surveys and other expenses related to the research. We also appreciate the assistance of Sekou Franklin in the tedious tasks of processing the survey data. The anonymous reviewer provided an incisive reading and critical evaluation of the manuscript, which resulted in improvements in its substance, organization, and style. We are grateful to Professor Hanes Walton Jr. of the University of Michigan for his critical reading and many helpful suggestions. We also thank Warner Davis for calling our attention to presidential-election chronicler's Theodore White's quote, which we use as the book's epigram. Finally, as always Smith is grateful to his wife, Scottie, for her work in preparation of the manuscript.

NOTES

1. The substantive and statistical meanings of our use of *gaps, gulfs,* and *chasms* in the study of racial differences in opinion in this study are discussed in chapter 1.

2. Seltzer's experience during the Simpson case was also shaped by the dynamics of a society divided by color, as he moved back and forth from a predominantly black workplace to a white home and a mostly white set of friends. Among his students at Howard, the vast majority thought Simpson was innocent, whereas his white friends universally accepted that he was guilty. And in two of the nonprofit organizations in which he worked as a consultant, it was decided by the senior staff to avoid discussion of the case because in the racially mixed workforce discussion was deemed too divisive and disruptive.

3. Half of the top-ten shows in black households were on the Fox network, whereas none of the top-ten white programs were on Fox (Carmen, 1996). A 1999 survey found that blacks and whites watched more of the same prime-time television shows than in 1995. Instead of one, there were four programs in the top-ten list of both black and white viewers: NFL *Monday Night Football, Touched by an Angel, 60 Minutes,* and the *CBS Sunday Movie.* However, the top-rated black program—*The Steve Harvey Show*—was ranked 154 among whites, and the top-rated white show—*ER*—was 18 in black households. See "Gap between Black and White TV Viewing Narrows," *Jet,* May 17, 1999a, p. 65.

4. Data from the *Los Angeles Times* exit poll as reported on CNN's "Inside Politics," April 8, 1997.

5. This suggests that academic surveys and commercial and media polls need to pay more attention to the attitudes and opinions of other Americans, not just of blacks and whites and not just of Latinos and Asian Americans, but of discrete national origin groups within these umbrella collectivities. Although it would be prohibitively expensive to oversample these groups routinely, it should be done occasionally because it would be useful to know the opinion of Latinos and Asian Americans on the Simpson case or any of the other controversies examined in this study.

6. Hochschild's paradox is in part a function of her grossly erroneous (misstated perhaps) view that blacks and whites have experienced the same history, live in the same society, and are affected by the same political events. The fallaciousness of this view should be obvious, but see chapter 1 for a discussion of the separate histories and cultures of blacks and whites in the United States, as well as their separate social, economic, and political circumstances.

1

Introduction

The scientific study of public opinion in the United States has its origins in the early polls conducted by Gallup and Roper in the 1930s.[1] With advances in questionnaire design and implementation, the advent in the 1950s and 1960s of the high-speed computer, and more-sophisticated sampling methodologies and techniques of statistical analysis, the study of public opinion has become one of the more advanced areas of research in the social sciences.

The early polls by Gallup and Roper as well as the early studies of public opinion by social scientists tended to ignore African Americans. Although there was a relatively large number of studies of racial attitudes and opinions on race, as Sigelman and Welch (1994: 1) wrote, in these studies of race opinion "blacks are conspicuous by their absence. These are books about white people's attitudes toward black people with only a passing glance toward the attitudes of blacks." During the civil rights movement, there were a few studies focusing on black opinion, including ten summary articles by Erskine that pulled together from commercial and academic survey organizations scattered survey items dealing with white racial attitudes and African American opinion on race and civil rights.[2] In their 1966 study of southern politics, Matthews and Protho surveyed the attitudes of blacks and whites; and the Brink and Harris (1964; 1966) surveys for *Newsweek* also focused on the attitudes of both races towrad race and civil rights issues. In 1964, Marx (1967) conducted interviews with 1,119 black adults, including a representative sample of 492 people living in metropolitan areas of the South and a representative sample of blacks living in Chicago, New York City, Atlanta, and Birmingham. This survey was concerned with understanding the sources and the strength of black militancy and nationalism in mass society. Thereafter "no national surveys focusing on blacks were done for fifteen years" (Sigelman and Welch, 1994: 2).

1

Many students of race opinion attribute this paucity of work on black opinion to the enormous influence of Gunnar Myrdal's 1944 book, *An American Dilemma*, on race relations research in the United States. Before turning to an examination of Myrdal's baneful influence on the study of race opinion in the United States, we first discuss briefly the meaning of public opinion.

THE MEANING OF PUBLIC OPINION

Like many of the terms used by social scientists, there is no precise, universally agreed definition of the term *public opinion* (Hennessy, 1985: 2). Lord Bryce said of public opinion that it is the "aggregate of views that men hold . . . that affect the community" (quoted in Walton and Smith, 2000: 62), whereas V. O. Key, in his classic *Public Opinion and American Democracy*, specifically linked the term to the government—that public opinion is those "opinions held by private persons which governments find it prudent to heed" (1961: 14). Hennessy, on the other hand, wrote that it is simply "the complex of preferences expressed by a significant number of persons on an issue of general importance" (1985: 8). Lane and Sears avoided the problem of definition altogether, assuming (presumably) that its meaning is a given. So they wrote that "opinions have to be *about* something" (1964: 2). And the something they said *public* opinion is about is (1) the political system, (2) the choice of group loyalties and identifications (race, religion, region, social class), (3) choice of leaders, and (4) public-policy preferences (2–3).

It is not our purpose in this book to engage in extended analysis of the meaning of the term. First, there is little we can add to what previous scholars have written; and public opinion is generally understood by scholars and the general public to mean the opinions of the public, or some segments of it, about issues of interest or importance to the society or some segments of it.[3] This usage calls attention to the fact, as John Dewey put it in *The Public and Its Problems* (1927), that there is not the public but rather public*s*, depending on issues, personalities, circumstances, and contexts. Second, public opinion may or may not involve topics or issues that the government should prudently heed (that is, the topic may be politically irrelevant). The issues also may be unimportant, trivial, but nevertheless of interest to the public. Public opinion, as Lane and Sears (1964) contend, may deal with government, leaders, policy issues, or group identities and loyalties. This working definition fits well the cases dealt with in this book. Some issues, like the O. J. Simpson case, are trivial but of enormous public interest; the topics of Farrakhan and Powell involve issues of leadership; the Persian Gulf War was an important policy issue; and cases like Barry, Brawley, and even Simpson deal with issues of race group loyalties and identifications.

EXORCISING THE GHOST OF GUNNAR MYRDAL
FROM RACE OPINION RESEARCH

Several scholars have pointed to the widespread influence of Myrdal's monumental two volumes on the study of race opinion specifically (McKee, 1993; Sigelman and Welch, 1994; Walton and Smith, 2000: chaps. 3–6) and race politics generally in the United States (Cox, 1959; Katznelson, 1971).[4]

In 1937 the Carnegie Corporation invited Myrdal, then a relatively unknown economist and a member of the Swedish Parliament, to come to the United States to conduct a major study of the nation's race problem. Myrdal had no prior interest in or experience with the subject. He was selected because of this, the feeling being that he could bring a tone of neutrality and objectivity to the study. Myrdal assembled a distinguished team of black and white scholars of race and, with unlimited time and money, examined virtually every aspect of the "Negro problem"—physiological, historical, psychological, cultural, economic, and political. The team's findings and conclusions became orthodoxy in the postwar study of race in the United States.

The report was widely read and recognized immediately as a classic; for social scientists it became the point of departure for research on race. James McKee (1993) wrote,

> *An American Dilemma* is the single most-renowned work in race relations . . . its status as a classic is undisputed. But this is not simply because of its size and comprehensiveness; these features do not alone win a place of honor in any body of literature. Rather, its classic status is due to the considerable influence it had at a time of generational change. Myrdal reviewed, summarized, and confirmed commonly accepted findings, thus reinforcing and legitimizing their status as knowledge. (225–26)

Myrdal saw America's race problem as a "white problem," a problem rooted fundamentally in the prejudiced attitudes of whites. Thus, in understanding race in America, white attitudes were hegemonic, whereas black attitudes were secondary, inconsequential. Myrdal wrote: "In the practical and political struggles of effecting changes, the views of white Americans are . . . strategic. The Negro's entire life and, consequently, also his opinions on the Negro problem are in the main to be considered as secondary reactions to more primary pressures from the side of the dominant majority" ([1944] 1962: 1143). In other words, there was no distinct or independent black opinion. Rather, "Myrdal believed that these secondary attitudes, being largely defensive responses to white attitudes and actions, were relatively superficial responses, not deeply rooted in the individual psyche or in cultural memory, and could easily be altered" (McKee, 1993: 232).

Until the 1980s, the ghost of Myrdal's paradigm haunted the study of African American mass opinion, resulting in relatively few studies of the phenomenon. Blacks were included in national polls and surveys in numbers reflecting their proportion of the population; but typically these surveys yielded too few respondents to produce valid and reliable findings or to explore opinion differences internal to the black community in terms of such things as gender, class, age, or region (the typical national sample of 1,500 to 2,000 people would include about 150 to 200 blacks).

The ghost of Myrdal was exorcised through a combination of factors: first, the growth and development of the African American studies discipline; second, the growing interest in African American society and politics in the traditional disciplines of political science and sociology; third, scholars' recognition of the radically erroneous nature of Myrdal's argument that black opinion is a mere derivative, secondary, transitory response to white opinion. It was gradually and even grudgingly recognized by the social science community that black opinion was worthy of study in its own right (Walton, 1985: chaps. 4 and 5; Gordon and Rollock, 1987).

As a result of these changes, survey and polling organizations began to conduct surveys specifically designed to study black opinion and to "oversample" the black population so as to provide samples of sufficient size to yield valid and reliable results and to permit the study of intragroup opinion within the black community. Altogether, these changes have led in the past decade (the 1980s) to "burgeoning research on race as an issue in American life" (Sniderman, 1993: 231).

THE LITERATURE ON RACE OPINION IN THE UNITED STATES

From the inception of the scientific study of American public opinion more than forty years ago, countless surveys have found that the American public is in general indifferent and uninformed about politics, political leaders, ideologies, and issues (Kinder, 1983; Sniderman, 1993). Very few Americans structure their opinions on politics in ideological terms, and their views on issues tend to be ad hoc, inconsistent, transitory, and often contradictory. These generalizations hold for virtually all issues—foreign and domestic—except, that is, for race.

In one of the classic studies documenting the lack of ideological or issue content in white-American mass opinion, Converse (1964: 238) wrote: "For the bulk of the mass public, the object with the highest centrality is the visible, familiar population grouping [Negroes] rather than abstract relations among parts of government and the like." More than thirty years later, Kinder and Sanders (1996: 14) also concluded that "compared with opinion on other matters, opinions on race are coherent, more tenaciously held and more difficult to alter . . . [white] Americans know what they think on matters of race."

White Opinion Research

The first thing to note about the race opinion of whites is that *it tends to be one of the few consistent anchors in the thinking of white Americans.*

Second, in the past thirty years, surveys have shown a steady and generally consistent decline in overt expressions of racist and white supremacist attitudes among white Americans (Condran, 1979; Harris, 1978; Schuman, Steeth, and Bobo, 1985; Smith, 1995: 39–42). For example, in 1963 31% of whites agreed with the statement that blacks were an inferior people; by 1978, only 15% agreed (Harris, 1978: 16). Studies have also shown that white Americans by large margins now embrace the *principle* of racial equality (see Schuman, Steeth, and Bobo, 1985; Sniderman and Hagen, 1985).

However, although white Americans in general are less openly racist in their attitudes toward blacks, this does not mean that hostility toward the race has disappeared or withered away. Instead, it has become less obvious, more subtle, more difficult to document. This new, more subtle form of racism has been labeled "symbolic racism," "modern racism," "racial resentment," and "laissez-faire racism" (Sears, Hensler, and Speer, 1979; Sears, 1988; Sniderman, Piazza, Tetock, and Kendrick, 1991; Kinder and Sanders, 1996: 272–76; Bobo, Klugel, and Smith, 1997). What this research purports to show is that white Americans are not racist in the old-fashioned way but instead resent or are hostile to blacks because of their commitment to basic or core American values, particularly individualism (Sniderman and Hagen, 1985). Sniderman summarized the research this way: "White Americans resist equality in the name of self-reliance, achievement, individual initiative, and they do so not merely because the value of individualism provides a socially acceptable pretext, but because it provides an integral component of the new racism" (1993: 232).

In this modern racism, blacks, according to whites, are not inferior and could get ahead in society, but they lack the initiative or drive to succeed. As a function of individualism, modern or symbolic racism is a product of the "finest and proudest of American values" (Sears, 1988: 54)—as American as the flag, baseball, the Fourth of July, and apple pie.

Blacks of course disagree, viewing racism and racial discrimination as the principal explanation for persistent inequalities between the races (Sigelman and Welch, 1994; Kinder and Sanders, 1996: 289; Hochschild, 1995: 55–90). Kinder and Sanders summarized this racial chasm: "Whites tend to think that racial discrimination is no longer a problem; that prejudice has withered away; that the real worry these days is reverse discrimination, penalizing innocent whites for the sins of the distant past. Meanwhile, blacks see racial discrimination as ubiquitous; they think of prejudice as a plague; they say that racial discrimination, not affirmative action, is still the rule in American society" (1996: 287). Finally, Hochschild (1995: 73) noted that "well-off, middle-class blacks tend to see more discrimination than poor blacks; see less of a decline in racism; expect less improvements in the future; and claim to have experienced more discrimination in their own lives." Reading these studies of how sharply the races differ on race almost makes surprise about the reactions to the O. J. Simpson verdict itself a surprise.

Black Opinion Research

The aforementioned studies are mainly about white people's opinion about race, with black opinions, as Myrdal's ghost would have it, secondary, derivative. There is, however, a small body of research that examined black opinion in its own right. These studies highlighted forces that shape the internal dynamics of black mass opinion.

In our work (Smith and Seltzer, 1992), we sought to determine the role of class in explaining racial differences in opinion and to explain the sources of intraracial differences in black opinion, focusing on such factors as gender, age, region (North-South), residence (urban-suburban), and marital status.[5] We found that on some attitudes there are few, if any, racial differences in political attitudes and behavior (attitudes on moral issues, family values, illegal drug use, and some forms of political participation), whereas on other attitudes the apparent race differences disappear when class is introduced (many types of political participation as well as political knowledge, interest, and efficacy, and attitudes toward the role of women in society). These results suggested that black and white Americans in general share a common civic culture.

But we also found three relatively distinct sets of racial attitudes, that is, differences between the races that persist even after controls for class were introduced or when blacks and whites of the same social class were compared. First, blacks of all social classes were found to be more religious than their white counterparts. Second, blacks were more alienated or distrustful of the government and other societal institutions as well as suspicious or distrustful of the motives of other individuals. Third, blacks were distinctively liberal, especially on issues of the economy and the welfare state.

Overall, what we showed in our 1992 book was that on many, many social and political questions there was no racial divide, especially among individuals in the same social class. The most striking documentation for our purposes in the 1992 work was the centrality of alienation and religiosity in structuring a distinctive black mass opinion.

Several other studies have documented the centrality of religion in structuring black mass opinion. Allen, Dawson, and Brown (1989), using the National Black Election Survey, found that a structurally distinctive African American belief system existed; that it was strongly influenced by religion; and that it helped process, constrain, and bias blacks' interpretation of reality.[6] In particular, this study showed that religiosity contributes to a strong sense of racial group identification and consciousness. Studies of the role of black religiosity show also that it contributes to political awareness, voting, and civic activism (Brown and Wolford, 1994; Reese and Brown, 1995; Harris, 1994). Religiosity therefore is perhaps a central source in distinguishing between white mass opinion and black mass opinion.

Other studies in black opinion have explored the sources of black voter identification with the Democratic Party and support for Jesse Jackson in his two campaigns for president, indicating that a strong sense of race group consciousness and solidarity are important factors (Gurin, Hatchett, and Jackson, 1989; Tate, 1994; Dawson, 1994). These studies also showed that although there is increasing class polarization in the black community, these class divisions do not significantly structure black partisanship, issue stances, or vote choices (Dawson, 1994). And when there is a class difference, it is poor rather than middle-class blacks who are likely to lean toward conservatism and the Republican party.

Finally, there is evidence of an increased level of black nationalist or separatist thinking in black mass opinion, especially among the poor and the young, although the most recent survey data also showed some increase among middle-class blacks (Dawson, 1995). Indeed, some scholars see a tendency toward "dual sovereignty" in black opinion, that is, views supportive of certain aspects of black nationalism as well as views supportive of certain "mainstream" values (Bobo, Klugel, and Smith, 1996).

We suspect that aspects of these distinctive elements of black opinion—religiosity, alienation, and nationalism—may serve as useful interpretative schemes for understanding aspects of black opinion on the cases and the controversies considered in this book.

THEORIES IN RACE OPINION RESEARCH

Theory, Sigelman and Welch wrote, "is not far advanced in race opinion research" (1994: 163). This is because it took so long to exorcise the ghost of Myrdal, and indeed Myrdal's ghost still lingers in some of the modern racism studies. Also, systematic surveys with adequate sample sizes—the building blocks of good empirical theory—have only been available since the 1980s.

In our work we advanced four theories that were helpful in explaining black-white opinion differences: (1) class; (2) "ethclass" (where race and class intersect because blacks tend to be disproportionately lower class and whites disproportionately middle class, making it difficult to separate the race–class effects on opinion); (3) cultural differences between the races; and (4) perceptions of differential group interest (Smith and Seltzer, 1992: 3–10).[7] Similarly, Kinder and Sanders (1996: 35–45) contended that "No Single Sovereign Theory Will Do";

rather, multiple theories or interpretative schemes or frames are needed to explain race opinion differences. They propose three theories: (1) race group interests, (2) race group sympathies and resentments, and (3) political principles (different group attitudes toward equality, the role of government, and individualism). They found these three theories to be useful in explaining some race opinion differences depending, they say, on how the issues are "framed"—framed by political leaders and the media in the course of the public debate and by social scientists and pollsters as they write survey questions.

It is a commonplace in the strategies of political consultants and the methodologies of social scientists that what the public thinks about an issue depends to some extent on how the issue is framed. This has been shown to be true on race opinions (Kinder and Sanders, 1996: 163–95). However, forty years of evidence suggest that race opinions tend to be somewhat more stable and deeply rooted than opinions on other issues. Thus, while we pay attention to the framing of the issues and the survey questions in this study, we also remain alert to the likelihood of opinion stability, no matter how the issue is framed in the public debate or in the survey questions.

DATA AND METHODS

In some sense our methodology and data nicely address the framing problem because this study involves not a single survey at a single point in time (as is frequently the case) but multiple studies at many points in time. Perhaps the best way to deal with the framing problem is to compare different kinds of issues using different questions at different points in time. This is our approach; yet continuity and fundamental context are maintained because most of the issues deal with race opinion.

We deal with a variety of issues and personalities, ranging across several time periods and several locales. Some of the issues are local whereas others are national. Some are trivial; others are of national significance. In addition, for many of the cases, we use multiple surveys. This makes for a uniquely rich, contextualized, and dynamic analysis of race opinion, unlike anything else in the literature.

Surveys and Polls

Forty-seven surveys or polls are used in the book, in addition to the 1996 General Social Survey. (See the appendix for a detailed list of the surveys, including information on the survey organization, the sample sizes, and the dates on which the survey or poll was administered.) Twelve polls are employed in our analysis of the Persian Gulf War, eight on various conspiracy theories, twelve on the Marion Barry case, six on O. J. Simpson, three on Rodney King and the L.A. riots, two each on Clarence Thomas and Louis Farrakhan, two on the Tawana Brawley case, and one each on Colin Powell and the Haitian crisis.

Gaps, Gulfs, and Chasms

The concept of a "gender gap" in opinion, partisanship, and vote choice between men and women is much more familiar to Americans than the "race gap," although relatively speaking the gender gap is trivial when compared to the race gap (Seltzer, Newman, and Leighton, 1997: 3).

A race gap, or more likely a gulf or a chasm, is as old as the American society, whereas the gender gap first emerged in public debate in 1980 when white male voters were somewhat more likely to support Ronald Reagan than white female voters. Although the data are not clear, it is possible that a gender gap has existed since women first got the vote in 1920 (Mueller, 1988). The survey data does show that a gender gap existed in the 1950s and the 1960s, when women were more conservative and more likely to vote Republican by margins of 8 to 9 points (Seltzer, Newman, and Leighton, 1997: 4).

Since 1980, women have tended to be somewhat more liberal and Democratic in vote choice than men, by margins of 5% to 10% (in the 1996 presidential election, it was 11%). Although there is no theoretically cogent explanation for this new phenomenon, it appears that it may be in part a function of women's somewhat greater concern for peace and social justice. In general, women, for example, are somewhat less likely than men to favor American military intervention abroad and cuts in social welfare, health, and education programs.

In this study we define a *race gap* as a statistically significant opinion difference between the races of 10 to 19, which at its outer limit exceeds any observed gender gap. A *race gulf* is an opinion difference of 20 to 39, and a *race chasm* is a difference of 40 or more.[8]

This is a study of opinion differences between blacks and whites. Based on the extant research, we expect to find race differences per se; that is, differences that in most cases are not explainable by class, age, gender, or anything else. However, where there are significant differences of class, gender, or age between or within the races, we will incorporate them into the analysis.

Finally, as in our previous book (Smith and Seltzer, 1992), in an effort to make the book accessible to the widest possible audience, we have attempted to present a narrative that is not unduly burdened with social science jargon and impenetrable statistical tables and analysis. Often in studies involving survey research, the methodology overwhelms the substantive product. This we try to avoid without compromising the integrity of the work and its value to specialists in opinion research or African American studies.

DIFFERENT WORLDS: HISTORICAL STRUCTURAL CONSIDERATIONS IN THE STUDY OF RACE OPINION

In her study of race differences in opinion, Hochschild (1992) remarked that it is paradoxical that African Americans and whites are so deeply divided on so many issues because, she argued, blacks and whites share the same history and the same social and economic experiences. This of course is grossly wrong. Perhaps Hochschild's point is poorly crafted because one does not have to be a social scientist specializing in the study of race (as she is) to know that blacks and whites do *not* share the same history and social and economic experiences in the United States. Rather, African Americans, as James Baldwin put it, inhabit "Another Country," with a radically different historical experience and memory—as different as day and night, as black and white, as slavery and freedom. Blacks also have radically different social, economic, and political experiences in the Untied States. As Malcolm X put it in his famous "Ballot or the Bullet" speech in 1964, blacks in America have not experienced the American dream; rather "I see only an American nightmare" (Breitman, 1966: 26). Thus, there is no paradox. Blacks and whites not only inhabit different "perceptual worlds" as Sigelman and Welch put it but also different real worlds, worlds that are separate and unequal (Hacker, 1992).

Most students of race opinion research (including Hochschild) include in their books a chapter or a section of a chapter documenting the large social and economic disparities between the races (Smith and Seltzer, 1992: 10–14; Sigelman and Welch, 1994: chap. 2; Dawson, 1994: chap. 2; Kinder and Sanders, 1996: 285–89). Smith and Seltzer also discuss the wide disparities in political status and power between the races. These scholars include this material in order to suggest that race opinion differences may be a function of structural inequalities between the races.

In understanding why blacks and whites frequently exhibit such deep divisions on many issues in America at the end of the twentieth century, we must consider not only structural asymmetries, because structural asymmetries are historically constructed, but also history and culture, because the distinctive histories of blacks and whites give rise to distinctive cultures. Berry and Blassingame (1982) titled their history of the black experience in the United States *Long Memory*. Black opinion at the close of the fourth century of their sojourn in America is in part shaped by this long historical memory; that is, some of their opinions are deeply rooted in both the individual psyche and the collective memory of blacks, as well as in their dissatisfaction with their separate and unequal status in contemporary American society.

Historical Considerations

The historically different worlds of blacks and whites should be too well known to require extensive discussion and documentation. If most Americans and students of race opinion are not familiar with the standard textbooks on African American history (Franklin, 1967; Bennett, 1967; Harding, 1981), they should be familiar with the telling of that history in such popular television programs as *Roots* and *Eyes on the Prize*.

In 1857 Chief Justice of the U.S. Supreme Court Roger B. Taney encapsulated the distinctive historical experience of blacks in the United States in his opinion in the infamous *Dred Scott* decision. He wrote:

> The question is simply this: Can a Negro, whose ancestors were imported into this country, and sold as slaves, become a member of the political community formed and brought into existence by the Constitution of the United States, and as such become entitled to all the rights, and privileges, and immunities, guaranteed by that instrument to the citizen? . . . We think they are not, and that they are not included, were not intended to be included under the word "citizen" in the Constitution and can therefore claim none of the rights and privileges that instrument provides for and secure to citizens of the United States. *On the contrary, they were at that time [1787] considered a subordinate and inferior class of beings, who had been subjugated by the dominant race, and, whether emancipated or not, yet remained subject to their authority, and had no rights or privileges but such as those who held the power and the Government might choose to grant them.* (emphasis added)[9]

More recently, writing in the context of a discussion of recent Supreme Court decisions hostile to affirmative action, Mack Jones, an African American political scientist, succinctly summarized the distinctive historical experience of blacks in the United States—the nightmare that Malcolm X referred to in 1964:

> The pertinent question [in discussing affirmative action] is should special consideration be given to individuals who belong to a group that was singled out for unequal treatment by the Constitution of the United States and by statutory law at all levels of government, national, state, and local, and whose unequal treatment was sanctioned by social custom and reinforced by the use of terror and economic intimidation and who, as a result of that government-mandated and culturally sanctioned oppression, lag behind white Americans on practically every indicator of socioeconomic well-being. The question is should members of that oppressed group receive special consideration until such time that the gap between them and the dominant group on these indicators of well-being are eliminated. (Jones, 1999: 249)

This history of subordination, subjugation, and oppression referred to by Chief Justice Taney and Professor Jones helped to shape a distinctive African American culture.

Cultural Considerations

Holden (1973: 17) wrote: "Since culture is behavior learned in cohorts, it follows that when two groups are separated by legal or behavioral frontiers over any significant time, some tendency toward cultural difference must develop." And Holden continued: "The obverse is also true, at the same time, if they coexist within the same linguistic, economic, or political system they must develop significant commonalities" (1973: 17). Holden's formulation is useful in calling attention to the fact that blacks in the United States share cultural commonalities with whites but also certain "partially distinctive attributes" that constitute a black culture (16).

The problems then are to identify those "partially distinctive attributes" that constitute black culture and shape contemporary black attitudes and behavior.

The first problem involves the idea of culture itself, a nettlesome, slippery concept that has defied a scholarly consensus on its meaning for generations. For example, fifty years ago Kroeber and Kluckhorn (1952) listed more than 150 relatively distinct definitions of *culture*. The time since then has hardly improved the situation. In a recent essay, one writer suggested that culture is used to explain almost everything and has been used so indiscrimately—"a culture of police conduct; a culture of racism; a culture of poverty; a culture of corporate aggression; a culture of permissiveness; a culture of capitalism; a culture of multiculturalism"—that it has reached the "point of meaninglessness" (Rothstein, 1999).

This is not the place to get into the complexities of defining culture. Suffice it to say here that when we refer to culture we are concerned with shared values, beliefs, and behavior that constitute the meanings of a way of living. To constitute a culture, these shared attitudes, values, and behaviors tend to be relatively stable and tend to cut across class, region, or other divisions to encompass the community as a whole.

The second problem is to identify those partially distinctive shared attitudes, values, and behaviors that distinguish African Americans in the United States. This too is a nettlesome, complex problem (see Huggins, 1971). However, there is a considerable body of scholarship that has identified several of these partially distinctive attributes that constitute the culture of blacks in the United States.

First, there is considerable evidence that racial group consciousness and identity is an important shared value among blacks (Hagner and Pierce, 1984; Dawson, 1994). Recent surveys show that more than 90% of blacks say they "feel close to black people in this country"; 69% say they share a common fate with other blacks.[10] Indeed, this race group consciousness and identification have an explicit component of black nationalism among some blacks—49% agree that "blacks form a nation within a nation," and 14% even go so far as to embrace the extraordinarily radical proposition that the United States should be formally divided into two nations, one white and one black.[11]

A second distinctive element of black culture is religiosity—an "Africanized Christianity." Genovese (1974: 280) described religiosity as the "Foundations of the Black Nation." Lincoln and Mamiya link religiosity to another important black cultural value, freedom. They wrote: "A major aspect of black Christian belief is found in the symbolic significance given to the word 'freedom.' Throughout black history the word 'freedom' found deep religious resonance in the lives and hopes of African Americans. . . . In song and deed freedom has always been the superlative value of the black sacred cosmos . . . God wants you free" (Lincoln and Mamiya, 1990: 4–5; see also Holden, 1973: 17–18).[12]

A wish for resistance or defiance of whites, and of white domination, is also a deep and profound value in black culture (Franklin, 1984). Holden wrote of this phenomenon that it is used

to compensate for the pervasive insults and humiliations of past and present by telling "the white man" where to go and what to do. . . . Defiant heroism is represented by the plantation folklore of the "bad nigger" or the "crazy nigger" who, pushed beyond his tolerance limits, retaliated with the simple self-help of personal violence, even if doing this guaranteed his death. (1973: 18)

A final component of black culture that is widely accepted by scholars of the subject is cynicism, suspiciousness, and alienation. This phenomenon of alienation and suspiciousness likely arises out of the shared history and experience of racial oppression. One of the marks of this oppression is an exploitative, subordinate environment in which one's life chances are manipulable and often manipulated by others, black and white. This certainly is true historically insofar as whites are concerned, given the legacy of the betrayal of the African in the United States from the signing of the Declaration of Independence down to the modern civil rights era. Thus, a relative suspiciousness of the motives of whites is part of the historical legacy of all blacks and probably continues to shape group attitudes. As Martin Luther King Jr. put it in his 1963 "I Have A Dream" oration, "America has given the Negro a bad check; it has come back marked insufficient funds,"

This theme is also central in the culture of African Americans in terms of black-on-black as well as black-white interactions. In the long memory of blacks, it is recalled that the three major slave rebellions of the antebellum era were betrayed by blacks (Kilson, 1964), thus, a relative suspiciousness of the motives of blacks as well as whites. As Frederick Douglass, the great abolitionist, put it: "The motto which I adopted when I stared from slavery was this—'Trust no man.' I saw in every white man an enemy; and [in] almost every colored cause for distrust" ([1892] 1968: 25).

Douglass's motto is found in black folklore with the character and symbol of the trickster (Dawson, 1967; Hampton, 1967) and it is an abiding motif of the blues (see Keil, 1966; Palmer, 1981). Of this cultural attribute in black folklore, Jones wrote:

> An examination of the folktales African Americans told one another shows a shrewd, self-centered individualism among the slaves, not the cooperative communalism seen by so much of the scholarship of the 1970s. Not a single Brer Rabbit story celebrates communalism. The Wily Hare is the archetypical individualist, always ready to put one over on foes or, if need be, on friends. (1990: 4)

As frames or lenses through which to view racial differences in opinion, these partially distinctive cultural attributes of African Americans are useful, as are the differences in the social and economic status of blacks and whites in the United States.

Structural Considerations

As we indicated earlier, most students of race opinion include statistical data comparing the social and economic status of blacks and whites because it is thought that these differences in the location of the two groups in the social structure partially account for the opinion differences. Even cultural differences between ethnic or racial groups may in part rest on socioeconomic differences. Van der Berghe wrote:

> Insofar as systems of ethnic relations are largely determined by structural asymmetries in wealth, prestige, and power between groups, an inventory of cultural differences are frequently symptoms rather than determinants of intergroup behavior, even in systems where the distinguishing criteria of group membership are cultural. (1967: 141)

Gaps, Gulfs, and Chasms

In addition to our inventory of historical and cultural differences, we look briefly at an inventory of social and economic gaps, gulfs, and chasms between blacks and whites.

The Education Gap

The historic education gap between blacks and whites has narrowed substantially since the end of the 1960s civil rights era. In 1960 43% of whites but only 20% of blacks were high school graduates; but by 1993 70% of blacks had graduated from high school compared to 84% of whites.[13] And among persons 25 to 29 years of age, the gap has virtually disappeared with black school graduation at 83% compared to 86% among whites. At the college level, 12.2% compared to 23.8% of whites in 1993 had earned a bachelor's degree or more. The college graduation gap is substantial, but it too has narrowed somewhat since the 1960s.

The Employment Gulf

In general, since the end of World War II, the ratio of unemployed blacks to whites has been two to one. In good times and bad times, this gulf has persisted, with blacks being twice as likely as whites to be looking for but unable to find a job. For example, in April 1999, when the unemployment rate declined to a near 30-year low, this gulf in joblessness between blacks and whites was unchanged— among whites, the unemployment rate was 3.8%; among blacks, 7.7% (Bureau of Labor Statistics, April 1999). And even when blacks are employed, there is a gulf between the races, with blacks disproportionately employed in the lowest job categories of operatives and laborers while being underrepresented in the highest professional and technical categories.[14]

The Income Poverty/Wealth Chasm

The income, poverty, and wealth differentials between blacks and whites are also large. In 1993 median, black-family income was $21,500, compared to $39,310 for white families. The ratio of black to white income is .55; meaning that, on average, black families have only 55% as much income as do white families. This chasm in income between the races has actually grown in the past three decades— in 1969, the ratio was .61.[15] In terms of poverty, there is also a chasm—in 1993, 31% of black families were below the poverty level, compared to 9% of white families.[16] And in their exhaustive study of the disparities in wealth between blacks and whites, Oliver and Shapiro (1995: 85–86) estimated that, on average, white Americans have nearly twelve times as much median net worth as African Americans ($43,800 versus $3,700). If one excludes equity in a house or a car and focuses only on financial assets such as stocks, bonds, and mutual funds, the wealth chasm becomes starkly black and white, as different as night and day, because black families have effectively no wealth, compared to an average of $7,000 for white families.[17]

The Residence Chasm

Although blacks and whites live in the same country, they disproportionately live in separate places, with whites tending to live in suburban enclaves and blacks remaining concentrated in the deteriorating core of the nation's central cities. The residential chasm is as large now as it was in the 1960s civil rights era. Massey and Denton (1988; 1990) estimated that in the typical American city 80% of blacks would need to settle in new neighborhoods in order to achieve integrated living patterns. Some of this residential chasm is a result of the socioeconomic differences between blacks and whites, but only *some*—Massey and Denton also show in their research that middle-class blacks are as segregated from whites as poor blacks. Thus, a large part of the residency chasm is also a function of a pattern of widespread discrimination against blacks (of all social classes) in the sale and rental of housing and in access to mortgage loans (Smith, 1995: 64–68). This residential segregation creates and sustains a "geography for race consciousness" in the United States (Gregory, 1998).

The Explanation Gap

Why do blacks have worse education, jobs, income, and housing than whites do? This question has in the past couple of decades been the focus of extensive social science research, and it has been asked in a number of polls and surveys (including the GSS). Thus, there are both popular and academic theories or explanations for the socioeconomic gaps, gulfs, and chasms.

Jones in the essay quoted earlier provided an unambiguous explanation for the disparities between the races, one that might be described as deriving from a black perspective. Jones (1999: 249) wrote that as a *result* "of government-mandated and culturally sanctioned oppression . . . [blacks] lag behind white Americans on practically every indicator of socioeconomic well-being." Jones's explanation is rejected by other scholars, black and white, who argue that attributes internal to the black community (psychological and cultural) are more responsible for present-day racial disparities than is racial oppression, past or present. (See Hernstein and Murray, 1994; Thernstrom and Thernstrom, 1998; see also Loury, 1985.)

These differing academic theories of the causes of black inequality have their counterparts in mass opinion. Since the 1980s, various polls and surveys have asked Americans their views as to why "on the average, blacks have worse jobs, income, and housing than whites." Although there are some within-group differences, in general, blacks tend to blame inequality on discrimination by a white-dominated society, whereas whites tend to downplay racial discrimination in favor of explanations that tend to focus on the shortcomings of blacks themselves (Sigelman and Welch, 1994: 67–109).[18]

CONCLUSION

Blacks in America do not share the same history, culture, and circumstances as whites do. Rather, blacks have relatively distinct histories and cultures, and they are and always have been less well-off than whites. As we indicated earlier in this chapter, scholars of race opinion have used multiple theories to explain the gaps and gulfs in opinion between blacks and whites. Each of these multiple theories has some explanatory value, as we will show in subsequent chapters, but we believe a full explanation and understanding of racial opinion differences requires appreciation of the different histories, cultures, and material circumstances of the two groups.

NOTES

1. The eighteenth-century French philosopher Jean-Jacques Rousseau in *The Social Contract* ([1762], 1955) is said to have been the first Western thinker to give extended thought to the relationship between public opinion and the government (see Speier, 1950). The modern study of the subject may be traced to the classic work of Lippman (1922).

2. Between 1962 and 1973 Hazel Erskine edited ten summary articles in *Public Opinion Quarterly* dealing with race, race relations, and civil rights. However, only one-third of these articles dealt specifically with African American opinion.

3. As Hennessey (1985: 2–3) pointed out, following Rokeach's (1968) work, it is useful to distinguish analytically between beliefs, attitudes, values, and opinions. *Opinions* are specific, frequently transitory views about something. *Beliefs* are more stable, enduring views. *Values* are the more important beliefs, and *attitudes* are general tendencies to respond to things in a predisposed way. In this work, the focus is on opinions and attitudes.

4. The principal criticism of Myrdal's approach to race relations generally is his view of the problem of black subordination as a moral problem or a dilemma rooted in individual prejudices rather than in power and politics. Katznelson wrote: "Myrdal's ethical-moral approach to prejudice begs the question: What are the social, economic, and political origins of relationships of racial inequality? What social, economic and political factors sustain such relationships?" (Katznelson, 1971: 62). In other words, a focus on the prejudiced attitudes of whites ignores the structural differences in the distributions of wealth, status, and power between blacks and whites that sustain racial inequality.

5. We used the University of Chicago's National Opinion Research Center's 1987 General Social Survey because it included a large oversample of 544 blacks, in addition to 1,323 whites.

6.   The National Black Election Survey was conducted by the Program for Research on Black Americans of the Institute for Social Research, University of Michigan. The surveys were conducted in 1984 and 1988 during the Jesse Jackson presidential campaigns. More than a thousand blacks were interviewed for each survey (see Tate et al., 1988; Tate, 1994: Appendix A).

7.   Smith (1988) in a study of six New York City ethnic groups—WASPs (White Anglo-Saxon Protestants), Irish, Jews, Dominicans, Cubans, Puerto Ricans, and African Americans—found that each of the theories had some explanatory value.

8.   Gaps, gulfs, and chasms are terms of art rather than scientific concepts; therefore precision is not possible. *Webster's New Collegiate Dictionary* defines a *gap* as a "separation in space" . . . "a wide difference in character and attitude." Relatedly, a *gulf* is "an unbridgeable gap"; a *chasm* is a "deep cleft" . . . [gorge] . . . "a marked difference or separation." Not exactly precise distinctions but suggestive of increasing degrees of difference.

9.   See *Dred Scott* 19 Howard (60 U.S.) 393, 1857, as cited in Kermit Hall, William Wiecek, and Paul Finkelman (eds.), *American Legal History: Cases and Materials* ((1991: 208).

10.   These data are from Katherine Tate, et al., *The 1984 National Black Election Study Sourcebook* (1988).

11.   These data are from Michael Dawson and Ronald Brown's "Black Discontent: The Preliminary Report of the 1993-94 National Black Politics Study," Report #1.

12.   Students of black culture almost universally agree that along with religiosity, music and dance are also integral components of black culture (Henry, 1990; George, 1989).

13.   Data comparing the social and economic status of blacks are drawn from the following census reports: *The Social and Economic Status of the Black Population in the United States: An Historical View, 1790–1978* (n.d.) and *The Black Population in the United States, March 1994 and 1993* (1995).

14.   For example, in 1994, 27% of white men and 38% of white women were in the professional and the technical job categories, compared to 15% of black men and 20% of black women. In the operatives and laborers categories, the distribution was 10% white men, 17% white women, 20% black men, and 27% black women (U.S. Bureau of the Census, 1995).

15.   The Census Bureau as well as other analysts attribute a large part of this increased income differential to an increase in the relative size of female headed households among blacks; such families earn only 28% of the income of black couple families. But even among female headed households there is a race chasm. Among blacks 49.9% are below the poverty level compared to 29.2% of white families headed by women (U.S. Bureau of the Census, 1995).

16.   In part as a result of the near unprecedented economic growth of the 1990s, the black poverty rate declined from 31% of black families to 26.5%. However, the racial disparity persisted as the poverty rate among white families also declined.

17.   Oliver and Shapiro (1995) make the useful point that when the annual lists of the highest paid Americans are published, they usually include several black athletes and en-

tertainers but that the much more significant and longer lists of the wealthiest Americans rarely, if ever, include a black person.

18. It should be clear that these are general racial group tendencies rather than fixed patterns. For example, Sigelman and Welch noted that "whites are split . . . and are becoming more open to the idea that whites themselves may be a cause of black problems. . . . [And] though many blacks reject these ideas, many do accept the notion that blacks are at least partially responsible for their inferior socioeconomic status in American society" (1994: 90, 93).

2

Race, Ideology, Partisanship, and Racialism

In this chapter we place the specific cases and controversies examined in this book in the broader or general context of public opinion in the United States. We rely on the University of Chicago's National Opinion Research Center's General Social Survey (NORC-GSS). The GSS has been administered either every year or every other year since 1972. Typically, the GSS includes a sample size of about 1,500, which yields too few blacks (about 150) to do any kind of detailed analysis of black opinion.[1] In 1994 NORC began conducting the GSS biannually with sample sizes of about 3,000. Thus it is now possible to conduct on a routine basis detailed study of black opinion.

The GSS, as the name suggests, is a *general* survey of opinion, including questions on politics, ideology, and public policy but also questions about opinion and behavior on an array of other activities and concerns of the public. In the 1996 survey, we analyzed more than four hundred questions. These questions covered virtually every public concern: religion and religious activities, family and gender issues, issues of sexuality, leisure activities, and social and economic status.

In this chapter we focus on issues of politics, ideology, public policy, and partisanship. First, it is these that constitute public opinion in the sense that V. O. Key and other political scientists understand the term; that is, they are opinions on matters to which government officials find it prudent to pay attention or heed.

Second, it is opinions on these issues about which blacks and whites are most sharply and deeply divided.

Table 2.1 shows the twelve categories of questions analyzed in the 1996 NORC-GSS. Of the twelve, only five show significant racial divisions: political/ideological, foreign policy, religion, alienation, and race. On the other categories of questions, the racial differences were either modest gaps or they disappeared altogether when controls for social class were introduced.

In other words, there is much more agreement between the races on the general or nonpolitical questions included in the GSS. For example, there were no or only modest differences between blacks and whites on questions concerning work and family life, child-rearing practices, sexuality, the legalization of drugs, gender issues, and leisure activities.[2] *Thus, although we focus on politics and ideology, where the races are divided, the reader should be aware that in general on social and lifestyle issues the country is not divided by color.* Opinion differences, where they exist on these questions, are in shades of gray rather than in black and white.

CONTINUING CULTURAL DISTINCTIVENESS: RELIGIOSITY AND ALIENATION

In our 1992 book, in addition to concluding that the black community was distinctively liberal when compared to the white community, we also found that the black community was distinguishable in two other ways: it was more religious, and it was more alienated. Our results in the 1992 study were based on the 1987 GSS; thus we briefly examine whether these distinctive attributes persist in the

Table 2.1   Categories of Questions from the 1996 NORC-GSS

Category	Number of Questions
Political/ideological	73
Civil liberties	38
Crime	12
Foreign policy	46
Religion	6
Alienation	95
Race	28
Children/family	19
Work/leisure	6
Gender	47
Sexuality	15
Miscellaneous	52
Total	437

1996 GSS, that is, whether there is, as we would expect, continuity in these cultural patterns.

The 1996 GSS asked questions on alienation and religiosity that replicate the 1987 survey items. Compared to whites, African Americans are more likely to indicate that they are strongly religious, pray more frequently, and believe that the Bible is literally true (see table 2.2). Blacks also are more likely to express opposition to the Supreme Court decision prohibiting school prayer. On all of these questions, the findings are consistent with what we observed in the 1987 survey (Smith and Seltzer, 1992: 30–31, 44–49, 86–88). The greater saliency of religion (specifically Christianity, the expressed religious faith of more than 90% of blacks) among black Americans is confirmed by answers to a new question on the 1996 GSS, which asked whether to be "truly American" one must be a Christian. Sixty-two percent of blacks agreed with this statement, compared to 36% of whites.

Blacks as a community are also more alienated than whites, as measured by

Table 2.2 Racial Differences in Religiosity and Alienation

	Blacks	Whites	Gap	Gulf	Chasm
Religiosity					
Strongly religious	46%	35%	11*		
Daily prayer	73	55	18		
Disapprove of Supreme Court school prayer decision	71	57	14		
Believe Bible literally true	56	27		29	
To be truly American/Christian	62	36		26	
*Alienation***					
People for themselves	69	54	15		
People take advantage of others	64	39		25	
People cannot be trusted	85	38			47
No sense planning for future	73	27			46

Source: General Social Survey, 1996.

*A race gap is a difference between the races of 10 to 19, a gulf is a difference of 20 to 39, and a chasm is a difference in excess of 40.

**The questions on alienation were worded as follows:

Would you say that most of the time people try to be helpful or that they mostly are just looking out for themselves?

Do you think most people would try to take advantage of you if they got a chance, or would they try to be fair?

Generally speaking, would you say that most people can be trusted or that you can't be too careful in dealing with people?

There is no sense planning a lot—if something is going to happen—it will.

trust in other persons, confidence in the institutions of American society, and a fatalistic perspective on life (on the definition and measurement of *alienation* used here, see Smith and Seltzer, 1992: 31–33). For example, on a principal measure of interpersonal alienation—whether one thinks in general that most people can be trusted—85% of blacks said no, compared to 38% of whites. African Americans are also more likely to take a fatalistic approach toward life, with 73% agreeing, for example, that there is "no sense in planning" because "what will happen will happen." Only 27% of whites agreed.[3]

As we argued in chapter 1, these differences between the races on religiosity and alienation may be viewed as "cultural attributes" that distinguish the races. We concluded in our 1992 work that these cultural residues when cojoined with the community's distinctive, interest-based liberalism provide an almost "outsider" character to African American political culture and communal life (Smith and Seltzer, 1992: 146–51). These cultural residues—especially alienation—provide a useful analytic frame of reference for interpreting some of the racial differences in some of the cases and controversies discussed later in this book.

LIBERALISM IS THE DECK, ALL ELSE THE SEA

The Reagan and the Bush administrations (and to a lesser but nevertheless significant degree the Clinton–Gore administration as well) sought to bring about a transformation in the context of the ideological, political, and policy debates in the United States (Smith and Walton, 1994; Walton, 1997). Their first objective was to discredit liberalism and to delegitimatize the role of government in the society and economy. This general attack on liberalism had racially specific components: first, to delegitimatize the black quest for racial justice through recurrent attacks on the "failed" government programs of the 1960s, affirmative action, and the welfare state; second, to reframe the policy debate on race from an emphasis on the responsibilities of government to a focus on the shortcomings of blacks themselves in terms of the absence of individual responsibility, "family values," and community self-help; third, to discredit the liberal black-leadership establishment and to create in its place an alternative or at least a competitive conservative black-leadership group.

In general, the conservative contextual transformation has been remarkably successful. Liberalism has been substantially discredited (at least among white elites and the white public), becoming the dreaded "L" word to be avoided by candidates with national political ambitions. Policy debate in general and on race in particular has indeed shifted to the right; race matters are now more frequently discussed in terms of black irresponsibility; and white mass opinion, as volatile and amorphous as it tends to be, appears to have followed this elite framing of ideology and policy debates.

However, to the extent that an element of the race-specific component of the attack on liberalism was to transform the black community's liberal inclinations, the conservative movement has met with little success. The conservative movement was able to manufacture a new conservative leadership formation, constituted by academics, pundits, radio and television talk show personalities, and appointed government officials (Conti and Stetson, 1989). This new conservative leadership formation, however, does not have a mass constituency in black America (no black conservative, for example, has been elected to Congress or to any other legislative seat from other than white-majority districts) or linkages with indigenous black institutions. And although the liberal black-leadership establishment has to some extent been discredited, this is as much a result of recurrent attacks from the black left and black nationalists as from the black right (Cruse, 1987; Reed, 1995; Smith, 1996).

The effort of the conservative movement to transform the left-liberal inclination of black mass opinion has had little success. On the contrary, as white mass opinion has shifted to the right since the 1980s, African American opinion appears to have become markedly more liberal.

In the post–Reconstruction era, when it was urged on blacks that they reconsider their partisan identification with the then liberal Republican Party (liberal in the sense that it favored government intervention to secure black civil rights and economic opportunity), Frederick Douglass, the preeminent black leader of the era, reportedly responded, "The Republican Party is the deck, all else the sea." The data from the 1996 GSS suggest that Douglass's response has been the response of African Americans to the most recent call for blacks to abandon ship. Although the ship of liberalism may appear to be sinking, African Americans are clinging to the deck.

CLINGING TO THE DECK

The fundamental or core cleavage between contemporary liberalism and conservatism in the United States is over the role of the federal government in the economy and society. In terms of public policy preferences, this core ideological cleavage translates into attitudes toward the size and the scope of the welfare state. Specifically this translates into preferences in terms of government spending to deal with a range of national problems and of raising the necessary taxes to pay for the expenditures. Liberals tend to favor relatively higher taxes and spending on domestic programs, which are seen as means to improve the living conditions of the people and to create a more egalitarian society. By these measures, African Americans are considerably and consistently more liberal than whites.

In table 2.3, data are displayed comparing black and white attitudes toward government spending on a variety of problems facing the nation. Specifically, the

Table 2.3   Racial Differences in Attitudes toward Government Spending, Selected Programs
(% Saying Spending Too Little or Right Amount)

	Blacks	Whites	Gap	Gulf	Chasm
Environment	75%	59%	16		
Health	81	66	15		
Cities	77	58	19		
Crime	82	67	15		
Drugs	78	58		20	
Welfare	42	10		32	
Social Security	71	49		22	
Parks	49	31	18		
Highways	35	39			
Improving Blacks' Living Conditions	85	26			59
Space	26	60		34	
Mean total spending gap between the races				16*	

Source: General Social Survey, 1996.

*Spending on race, space, and highways is excluded—race because the huge chasm distorts the mean, and space and highways because blacks favor less spending.

question asked was whether the government was spending "too much money on it" (the program or problem), "too little money" or "about the right amount." We classify as liberal responses that indicate too little or right amount. Of the ten programs or policy areas, black respondents gave the liberal response on all except two: highway spending and space exploration.[4] The differences on highway spending are modest (39% of whites, compared to 35% of blacks, say too much or about right); however, spending on space represents a gulf between the races— 60% of whites indicate spending is too little or about right, compared to 26% of blacks (a gulf of 34). The 1996 GSS did not ask a question about defense spending; but in its previous surveys, a racial gulf similar to the one on space was observed. What this shows is that blacks tend to favor spending on programs devoted to improving the living conditions of people rather than infrastructure, the military, or space exploration.

The chasm in opinion on government spending, not surprisingly, is toward spending to "improve the living conditions of blacks"; 26% of whites but 85% of blacks say too little. Again, this chasm of 59 between the races is not unexpected. But as table 2.3 shows, there are gaps and gulfs in every area of domestic spending, from the environment to parks, from health to welfare. As a summary measure, the table includes the mean, or average, support among blacks and whites for spending on all of these programs (excluding race, highways, and space), showing a race gap of 16.

To put this point in perspective, we compare the race gulf with the gender differences among whites. In table 2.4, we see a gender gap only for spending on

Table 2.4   Gender Differences among Whites in Attitudes toward Government Spending, Selected Programs (% Saying Too Little or Right Amount)

	Men	*Women*	*Gap*
Environment	60%	57%	
Health	62	69	
Cities	54	57	
Crime	65	69	
Drugs	60	56	
Welfare	63	64	
Social Security	46	52	
Parks	34	27	
Highways	7	9	
Race	25	27	
Space	69	52	17
Mean gender difference	5		

Source: General Social Survey, 1996.

space (17), with women favoring less spending. In all other areas, the differences between white women and men (2–7) are negligible or trivial, with a mean difference of 5. Among African Americans, there also is no gender gap. Nor are there statistically significant[5] differences among the races based on social class.

The GSS further measured the government-spending issue by linking support for increased government spending to higher taxes to see whether this alters opinion. It does not. As table 2.5, shows the race difference persists in support for increased government spending on domestic programs even when respondents are told, "It might require a tax increase to pay for it." In each area, blacks favor increased spending when compared to whites; but in the area of unemployment, the difference constitutes a chasm of 48. The mean or average difference between the races is a sizeable gulf of 30.

Table 2.5   Racial Differences in Attitudes toward Government Spending on Selected Programs—Even If Tax Increase Required (% Agreeing)

	Blacks	*Whites*	*Gap*	*Gulf*	*Chasm*
Health	87%	64%	23		
Schools	54	25	29		
Retirement benefits	79	46	33		
Unemployment benefits	69	21			48
Culture and arts	68	51	17		
Mean race gulf				30	

Source: General Social Survey, 1996.

Table 2.6   Racial Differences in Attitudes toward the Social Welfare Responsibilities of Government (% Saying Government Responsibility)

	Blacks	Whites	Gulf	Chasm
Jobs	74%	33%		41
Health care	69	33	36	
Decent standard of living	70	33	37	
Decent living for unemployed	77	43	34	
Income inequality	73	44	29	
Financial aid to college students	62	30	32	
Decent housing for all	50	14	36	
Mean race gulf			35	

Source: General Social Survey, 1996.

Let us examine two other measures that tap the ideological cleavage between the races. The data in table 2.6 show attitudes toward the role of the federal government in assuring the health and well-being of the people. Is the government's responsibility to assure the availability of jobs, health care, housing, a college education, or an overall decent standard of living? On each of these items, there is a race gulf of 30 or more; and for employment, the race difference is a chasm of 41, with 74% of blacks favoring a government role and only 33% of whites. The mean, or average, difference on these questions is a gulf of 35.

The left-right ideological cleavage between the races is obviously wide and deep. There is even substantial support among African Americans for moving beyond liberalism toward aspects of democratic socialism. Table 2.7 compares race differences in opinion toward government ownership of selected private enterprises—electric utilities, hospitals, and banks. Again, substantial gulfs are observed. For example, 59% of blacks favored government ownership of hospitals, and 47% favored ownership of banks (20% and 18% of whites, respectively). The mean difference on these socialist indicators is a gulf of 29.

Table 2.7   Racial Differences in Attitudes toward Government Ownership of Selected Private Enterprises (% Favoring Government Ownership)

	Black	Whites	Gulf
Electric utilities	39%	17%	22
Hospitals	59	20	39
Banks	47	18	29
Government should reduce income differences between rich and poor	73	44	29
Mean race gulf			29

Source: General Social Survey, 1996.

Finally, blacks are more likely to agree that it is the government's responsibility to promote an egalitarian society by reducing income differences between the rich and the poor—73% of blacks compared to 44% of whites (a gulf of 29).

These gulfs and chasms in opinion differences between the races on the role of government in society and on tax and spending policies translate into differences in partisan preferences and electoral choice. In the 1996 presidential election, like all previous ones since 1964, African Americans favored the more liberal of the two parties and candidates. ("More liberal" is the appropriate phrase because the Democratic Party in recent years has not been so liberal in terms of the issues discussed here.) These race differences constitute chasms. The gulf in party identification in the GSS is 36 (77% of blacks identify with the Democratic Party, 41% of whites). And the difference in presidential choice is a chasm of 49 (92% of blacks voted for Clinton, 43% of whites).

African American adherence to liberalism in the United States is historically and structurally rooted.[6] Historically, it was an activist federal government that liberated blacks from slavery in the 1860s, restored their civil rights in the 1960s, and provided a measure of economic and social security during the 1860s, 1930s, and 1960s. And when the federal government retreated from its activist roles in the 1860s post–Reconstruction era and the 1960s post–civil rights era, the status of blacks also declined.

The structural roots of black liberalism are found in real or perceived race group interests on the part of both the black middle class and the poor. African Americans are disproportionately poor, jobless, and without adequate housing and health care. Thus, logically in terms of self-interest, it follows that poor blacks would favor an expansive welfare state that provides a decent standard of social well-being for all persons. But what about middle-class blacks? Ideologues of the conservative movement have argued that middle-class blacks share a common interest with their white counterparts in relatively lower taxes and spending. But most middle-class blacks reject this class-based conception of interests. Instead, their adherence to liberalism is in part cultural—a function of historical memory and of a sense of linked fate with poor blacks, a sense of being a part of a racially defined community. There is also a structural or economic basis for middle-class black liberalism. The post–civil rights era black middle class is disproportionately employed by the government, especially in its social welfare and educational bureaucracies. As Charles Hamilton has pointed out, "Basically, the black middle class is salaried from the public sector, and this circumstance largely determines the sort of hard self-interest positions this class will take on certain public policy issues" (quoted in Poinsett, 1973: 36). Therefore, in black America in the late twentieth century, there is a kind of "historical cultural–structural liberalism" that bridges class and status differences to foster an ideologically homogeneous or monolithic community.

RACE MATTERS

The 1996 GSS included a series of questions dealing with race-specific issues and relations between the races generally. Although one might expect on issues of race that the black–white cleavage would be at its widest, in general this is not the case. Rather, the differences between the races on these race matters are no larger (and are frequently smaller) than the ideological differences discussed in the preceding sections.

School Busing and Affirmative Action

At the end of the civil rights era, two issues came to dominate the discussion of race and public policy. First, from the late 1960s until the late 1970s, the issue was busing for purposes of school desegregation. And since the late 1970s, the issue has been affirmative action. Both issues have resulted not only in gulfs and chasms between black and white opinions, but also in significant differences in opinion within the black community. A brief discussion of the historical development and evolution of these two issues provides a context for understanding contemporary opinion.

When the Supreme Court in its famous 1954 decision *Brown v. Board of Education* declared that segregated schools were unconstitutional, it did not order that schools be desegregated. Rather, a year later in what is called *Brown II*, the Court ordered the states practicing segregation in public education to desegregate with "all deliberate speed." In other words, the states were told to take their time, to desegregate the schools but to do it slowly. It was not until 1969 in *Alexander v. Holmes County Board of Education* that the Court ordered the states to desegregate the schools "at once."[7] It was only after this decision—some fifteen years after *Brown*—that most southern schools began to desegregate their separate and unequal schools.

In 1971 in *Swann v. Charlotte-Mecklenburg Board of Education*, the Court ordered school districts to use busing in order to achieve racial balance or quotas so that "pupils of all grades be assigned in such a way that as nearly as practicable the various schools at various grade levels have about the same proportion of black and white students."[8] Then in *Keyes v. Denver School District No.1* (1973), the Court ruled that even if a school district had never practiced de jure (legal) segregation, it could violate the principles of *Brown* by practicing de facto segregation, that is, segregation in practice or fact. Specifically, in a seven-to-one ruling, the Court held that although Denver had never maintained de jure segregation, it had deliberately created a separate and unequal school system through a strategy of locating schools and drawing boundary lines in such a way as to place blacks in separate schools with the oldest books and the least-experienced teachers.[9] The Court then ordered, as it had in *Swann*, that Denver bus black and white students so as to achieve racial balance in all of its schools. The principles of *Keyes* were soon applied nationwide, leading to an enormous political controversy and eventually to a decision by the Supreme Court to reverse its position and put an end to school busing.

In many cities court-ordered busing led to mass protests by whites, to boycotts and violence, and to "white flight" to private or suburban schools. George Wallace, Richard Nixon, and Ronald Reagan made opposition to busing a major theme in their presidential campaigns; and both conservative and liberal members of Congress, from the north and the south, began to introduce legislation to stop the courts from ordering busing. Presidents Nixon and Ford proposed similar legislation, and in 1974 the House passed by a vote of 281 to 128 a bill prohibiting the courts from ordering busing for purposes of school desegregation. The Senate in a narrow 47-to-46 vote rejected the House bill and instead adopted an amendment prohibiting busing unless the courts found that it was "needed to guarantee a black child his constitutional rights"—a prohibition that in effect transformed the House bill into a nonbinding suggestion to the courts (Rich, 1974).

In *Milliken v. Bradley* (1974) the Supreme Court, however, took the Senate's suggestion and began the process of dismantling busing for purposes of desegregation. Specifically, the Court overturned a lower court order that required busing between largely black Detroit and its largely white surrounding suburbs. The Court majority agreed that Detroit's schools were unconstitutionally segregated but held that cross-district busing between city and suburb was not required to comply with *Brown*.[10] In an angry dissenting opinion, Justice Thurgood Marshall (the Court's only black and the attorney who argued *Brown* in 1954) accused his colleagues of bowing to political pressure and of being unwilling to enforce school busing because it was unpopular with the white majority.

Since *Milliken*, the Court has continued to retreat from busing as a device to desegregate the schools. In Denver, for example, although the schools are more segregated now than when the *Keyes* decision was handed down in 1973, a federal judge (with the approval of the Supreme Court) has allowed the city to abandon its twenty-year-old school busing program and return to neighborhood schools (Brooks, 1995).

Because of "white flight" to the suburbs, America's urban school systems cannot be desegregated unless there is cross-district busing between city and suburbs. The Supreme Court, however, will not permit this. Thus, forty years after *Brown*, most African American school children remain in schools that are separate and unequal.[11]

From its start, as a public policy busing was enormously unpopular. From the beginning of polling on the issue in the 1970s, white support for busing never exceeded 25%. But black opinion on the policy was also marked by gulfs and chasms during the 1970s and 1980s, never exceeding 60% support (Sigelman and

Welch, 1994: 123–26). Although busing has been replaced by affirmative action as the most-salient race policy issue in the 1990s, it remains racially divisive, as the data in table 2.8 show. It is supported by only 24% of whites and 59% of blacks (a black-white gulf of 35, but also large differences among blacks). Consistently throughout the 1960s, blacks (as well as whites) overwhelmingly agreed that "it is more important to improve schools in black neighborhoods than to bus to achieve racial integration" (Sigelman and Welch, 1994: 126).

Affirmative action as a racial public policy had its origins in the Kennedy-Johnson and Nixon administrations (see Graham 1990: 278–345). More specifically, in their present forms, affirmative action policies may be traced to the Nixon administration's "Philadelphia Plan" (so-called because it was originally designed to correct the underutilization of blacks in that city's construction industry) and to the Supreme Court's decision in *Regents of the University of California v. Bakke* (1978).

In 1970, President Nixon issued Executive Order No. 1246. It required all businesses with contracts with the government in excess of $50,000 and with fifty or more employees to develop an affirmative action plan that would include (1) an analysis of all job categories to determine the underutilization of minorities (*underutilization* defined as having fewer minorities in a particular job category than would reasonably be expected by their availability in the relevant labor force) and (2) a specific plan with "goals and timetables" to correct any underutilization identified. This order became the model for affirmative action programs at all levels of government and in private industry, as well as in college and university admissions.

Affirmative action policies permit the government and other institutions to take race (and gender and ethnic minority status) into account in order to give special considerations, preferences, or set-asides to individuals from disadvantaged groups.

Table 2.8   Racial Differences in Attitudes toward Busing for Purposes of School Desegregation and Racial Preferences in Hiring and Promotions

	Black	*Whites*	*Gulf*
Busing	59%	24%	35
Racial Preferences	50	11	39
Whites Likely to Lose Job/Promotion Because of Racial Preferences[*]	50	76	26

Source: General Social Survey, 1996.

[*]The question read: Some say that because of past discrimination, blacks should be given preference in hiring and promotion. Others say that such preference in hiring and promotion of blacks is wrong because it discriminates against whites. What about your opinion—are you for or against preferential hiring and promotion of blacks?

The purposes or justifications for these programs are (1) to remedy or to compensate these groups for past discrimination, (2) to enforce or implement the anti-discrimination provisions of the 1964 Civil Rights Act, and (3) to create diversity in education, employment, and government contracts. The fact that these programs permit the consideration of race in allocating benefits raises the question of whether this is constitutionally permissible or whether, as the critics suggest, the Constitution should be "color-blind."

This question was presented to the Supreme Court in 1978 in *Bakke*.[12] The case involved two questions: (1) Was it constitutionally permissible for a state to take race into account in allocating material benefits, in this specific case access to medical school? (2) If the use of race was permissible, could the state use a numerical racial quota (in *Bakke* this involved setting aside 16 of 100 slots for minority students only)? In deciding the case, the Court was deeply divided, issuing six separate opinions. Four conservative justices led by Justice William Rehnquist argued that the University of California program violated Title VII of the 1964 Civil Rights Act (which prohibits discrimination by institutions receiving federal funds) and the equal protection clause of the 14th Amendment. In their view, it was never permissible to take race into consideration in allocating material benefits. Four liberal justices led by Justice William Brennan and Justice Thurgood Marshall held that a state, in order to remedy past discrimination or to create ethnic diversity, could take race into consideration in allocating benefits and could, if it wished, use a fixed quota. Justice Lewis Powell, the Court's only southerner, split the difference between his liberal and conservative colleagues by holding that a state could use race for purposes of diversity but that a fixed quota was illegal and unconstitutional—in other words, affirmative action yes, quotas no.

Like busing, affirmative action generated enormous controversy and debate.[13] And like busing it created gulfs and chasms in opinion between blacks and whites, as well as among blacks. And finally like busing—given the state of public opinion—the Supreme Court, if not the Congress, is likely to do away with it.[14] This is because in the American democracy a policy as unpopular among the majority as affirmative action probably cannot be long sustained, especially because its presumed major beneficiaries—blacks—are themselves divided.[15]

From 1970 to 1995, white support for affirmative action (when defined in terms of racial preferences) has never exceeded 20%, whereas black opinion has always exceeded 40% (Steeth and Krysan, 1996). The data reported in table 2.8 essentially replicate this pattern of opinion. Only 11% of whites but 50% of blacks support affirmative action. The black-white difference is a near chasm of 39; but among blacks, opinion is also divided. Related to this, 76% of whites and 50% of blacks agree that the chances are good that whites will not get a job or promotion because of affirmative action—again, a black-white gulf, but also large differences of opinion among blacks.[16]

Explanations of Racial Inequality

As pointed out earlier in this chapter, the conservative movement sought to change the context of the debate on race in America. Throughout the 1980s and 1990s, conservative scholars, journalists, and politicians, both black and white, advanced the argument that blacks in general have fewer material resources (in terms of education, jobs, income, etc.), not because of racism or discrimination but because of their own shortcomings as individuals and as a community. As the argument goes, other ethnic groups have faced discrimination and overcome it, so—unless something is wrong with them—why can't blacks (see Salins, 1996, for a recent statement of this argument).

We pointed out in chapter 1 that there is a tendency for blacks to blame racism for their lower status in America, whereas whites tend to blame blacks themselves. But we noted that this was a tendency rather than a fixed pattern because there are divergences and convergences between the groups. The data in table 2.9 illustrate these tendencies, divergences, and convergences. Most whites (52%) see a lack of individual motivation rather than discrimination as the "main" cause of the lower status of blacks, whereas 64% of blacks see past discrimination as the main cause. Thus, we observe here a modest gap on individual motivation and a gulf on past discrimination. However, on the other possible "main causes," the differences are nonexistent (only 10% of both races accept the Hernstein and Murray, 1994, thesis of innate black inferiority) or modest gaps of 10 or so on the role of education or the lack of motivation or willpower. On the motivation question, the differences among blacks are larger than the black-white gap of 11.

The table also shows that whites are much more likely than blacks to say that the conditions of blacks have improved in recent years—65% to 36%—a gulf in perceptions of 29. Finally, 77% of whites agree that if the Irish, Jews, and other groups overcame prejudice and "worked their way up," so should blacks. Only 54% of blacks agreed. But, the intraracial difference is again greater than interra-

Table 2.9   Racial Differences on "Main" Causes of Black Inequality

	Blacks	Whites	Gap	Gulf
Past discrimination	64%	35%		29
Lack of individual motivation	41	52	11	
Lack inborn intelligence	10	10	—	
Lack of chance for education	54	45	—	
Blacks should overcome prejudice;				
work their way up like Irish, Jews, etc.	54	77		23
Conditions of blacks improved in recent years	36	65		29

Source: General Social Survey, 1996.

cial difference. It appears that the conservative framing of this aspect of the issue has considerable support in public opinion among both blacks and whites.

Racial Identities and Identifications

As indicated in chapter 1, identification and a sense of shared fate with "the race" is an attribute that distinguishes African American culture in the United States.

"Whiteness" and "White Studies" have of late become popular—something of a fad—in the academy. Some of the studies in whiteness have made intriguing contributions to our understanding of the social construction of whiteness and in analysis of the ideology of white supremacy and white skin privilege. (For studies in whiteness see Ignatiev, 1995; Ignatiev and Garvey, 1996; Dryer, 1999. See also *Transition*, Issue 73.) But, while whiteness may be important to the identities of American whites, it is not embraced in the same or the explicit way that blackness is among African Americans, with the exception (to some extent) of southern whites (Hulbert, 1989; Reed, 1983). Blackness is more of a cultural value for blacks than whiteness is for whites; at least this is the inference from the available survey data.

Data in support of this inference is shown in table 2.10. A large majority of blacks (65%, compared to 34% of whites) say they feel "very close" to their race or ethnic group—a race group identification gulf of 31.[17] Blacks are also more favorable toward government aid to minorities to preserve their traditions and customs, 45% to 11%.

Racial identities and identifications in some instances help to shape black opinion on controversial figures like O. J. Simpson and Marion Barry and on cases like the Rodney King beating and verdict.

SUMMARY

Although there is evidence of greater solidarity among blacks on race matters, there are also significant differences among blacks that should not be overlooked.

Table 2.10   Racial Differences in Attitudes toward Race Group/Ethnic Solidarity

	Black	Whites	Gulf
Feel close to race/ethnic group	65%	34%	31
Government should aid in preservation of ethnic/minority cultures	45	11	34

Source: General Social Survey, 1996.

In addition, on most matters of a general, nonpolitical nature (family, work, leisure, sexuality) opinion differences between the races are modest or nonexistent. Opinion differences between blacks and whites are most marked where they count, on ideology and partisanship. African American and white American opinions are marked by large gaps, gulfs, and chasms across the left–liberal ideological divide. The 1996 GSS indicates that the races are as divided, if not more so, on the left-right cleavage as they are on several important race issues. Indeed on several race matters, the divisions are larger among blacks than they are between blacks and whites.[18]

NOTES

1.   In 1987 the GSS included a special oversample of 544 blacks, which allowed us in our 1992 book to conduct detailed intraracial analysis of black opinion.

2.   Blacks are more likely than whites to report frequent television viewing, 74% to 48%.

3.   Although blacks are less likely to express confidence in selected American institutions than whites are, the differences are modest. For example, the mean difference between blacks and whites was 12 for a "great deal" of confidence in the following institutions: major companies, the Supreme Court, the scientific community, and the army. Majorities of whites and blacks did not have a great deal of confidence in any major American institution; however, blacks had greater confidence in organized religion—34% to 25%.

4.   We classify support for spending on highways and space as liberal only in the sense that there is support for increased government spending and that liberals in general favor increased government expenditures, except for the military. However, many modern liberals object to spending on space because it is viewed as military related rather than pure science. Liberals also argue that money spent on space exploration could be better spent on earth and that money spent on more and more highways damages the environment.

5.   A difference that is not statistically significant is one that could have occurred by chance.

6.   These arguments about the historical and structural roots of African American liberalism are developed in greater detail in Smith and Seltzer (1992:120-24).

7.   392 U.S. 430 (1969).

8.   402 U.S. 1 (1971).

9.   413 U.S. 189 (1973).

10.   418 U.S. 717 (1974).

11.   For a good collection of papers that provide a summary and overview of the legal and political issues in the busing controversy, as well as research on the effects of school desegregation on the educational attainments of black and white students, see Mills (1973).

And for a study of the effects of the Supreme Court's decisions dismantling busing on the increasing segregation of the schools, see Orfield (1996).

12. *Regents of the University of California v. Bakke*, 438 U.S. 265 (1978).

13. For an overview of this debate, see Curry (1996) and Davis (1995).

14. In the past several years, a narrow, conservative five-person majority has rendered several decisions that effectively undermine affirmative action. It is widely believed that the current conservative majority, when it is faced with a case raising facts similar to *Bakke*, will also reverse this precedent. For analysis of recent Supreme Court jurisprudence on affirmative action, see Walton and Smith (2000: chap. 13). It should also be noted that voters in several states (including California) have abolished affirmative action by ballot. However, the Republican-controlled House and Senate in 1998 by narrow margins rejected attempts to abolish affirmative action in higher education programs and government contracting.

15. Actually, the available research indicates that white women are the major beneficiaries of affirmative action (Leonard, 1984; Sims, 1995). But, alas, white women are almost as opposed to affirmative action as white men are.

16. Sigelman and Welch (1994) attributed the relatively low level of support of affirmative action among blacks to their adherence, like whites, to the strong strain of individualism in American liberal culture and to their support for the principle of merit in the allocation of resources. On the powerful effects of individualism in American culture and its effects on race reform, see Cochran (1999).

17. Black men (80%) and older blacks (82%) are more likely than black women (65%) and young blacks (64%) to indicate that they feel close to the race.

18. Two additional recent examples where black-white differences on race matters are greater than intrablack differences involve attitudes toward slavery. (1) In early 1997 Congressman Tony Hall, a white Democrat from Ohio, proposed that Congress formally apologize to blacks for slavery, a proposition that was supported by 67% of blacks and opposed by 65% of whites. (2) There is a nascent movement among blacks to ask the U.S. government to pay reparations for slavery (see Lumumba, Obdele, and Taifa, 1995), as was done for Japanese Americans for their confinement during World War II. This idea was supported by 65% of blacks and opposed by 88% of whites. These survey results were reported on ABC's *Nightline*, July 7, 1997.

3

American Foreign Policy and the Persian Gulf War

The opinions of African Americans on international affairs and U.S. foreign policy have not been given much attention by students of public opinion or of African American politics. Compared to the studies of black opinion on domestic issues and the related works comparing black and white opinion differences, we know hardly anything about the foreign policy views of blacks or how they compare to those of whites. For example, of the several major book-length studies of race opinion discussed in the preface and chapter 1, not a single one devotes any attention to foreign policy and international affairs.

The absence of research on African American foreign policy opinion is a part of the larger problem of the neglect by historians and political scientists of the roles of blacks in the country's foreign relations. This neglect of blacks' roles in international affairs and their opinions probably reflects to some extent the view—the bias—that although blacks might have a role in and opinions on domestic issues, especially race and civil rights, they have no interest or role to play in foreign policy. This was the view expressed by the nation's leading newspapers when Dr. Martin Luther King Jr. decided to join in leadership of the Vietnam War protests during the 1960s.

Despite this scholarly neglect, blacks have attempted almost from the beginning of the republic to play a role in international affairs. As Walton and Smith (2000: 280) wrote:

In their quest for universal freedom African Americans, who were born in foreign affairs through African slavery and the slave trade, have turned to America's foreign

39

policy to support policies of human rights and humanitarianism. An appreciation of the universal freedom thrust of African American politics must include an under-standing of African Americans' role in foreign policy.[1]

In this chapter, we first examine racial differences in foreign policy opinion in general. For this purpose, we use the Chicago Council on Foreign Relations (CCFR) 1994 survey of American foreign policy opinion. The 1994 survey, the most recent available at the time of our writing, has a relatively large sample of 1,492 people.

We follow this general analysis with case studies of two recent foreign policy controversies: (1) the Persian Gulf War and (2) the situation of the Haitian refu-gees and the efforts of the Clinton administration to restore the democratically elected president—Jean Bertrand Aristide—to power after his ouster in a military coup. Our analysis of the Haitian controversy is brief, relying on a single poll conducted by the *Washington Post/ABC News* at the height of the crisis.

Our study of the Persian Gulf War is much more detailed, relying on twelve surveys conducted by the *Washington Post/ABC News*. These twelve polls were administered between August 1990 (within a week of the Iraqi invasion of Ku-wait) and March 1991, immediately after the cease-fire. Having such a large number of surveys and a near year-long time frame allows us to engage in dy-namic opinion analysis, focusing on stability as well as change.[2]

FOREIGN POLICY OPINIONS OF BLACKS AND WHITES

The CCFR survey first asked respondents a general question regarding interest in news about other countries and international relations as compared to their inter-ests in news about local, state, and national politics. As shown in table 3.1, only

Table 3.1   Racial Differences in Attitudes and Interest in Foreign Policy

	Blacks	Whites	Gap
Interest in news about (% say very interested)			
Local Community	65%	67%	—
State	52	45	—
Nation	48	57	—
Other countries	31	34	—
Relations of U.S. with other countries	42	52	10
Impact of foreign policy on personal life (% saying major impact)	56	40	16

Source: Chicago Council on Foreign Relations, American Public Opinion and U.S. Foreign Policy, 1994.

modest differences existed between the races. Although whites are somewhat more interested in news about the relations of the United States with other countries, there is not a statistically significant difference in terms of news about other countries, with about a third of respondents indicating they follow the news about other countries. The data in the table confirm the not surprising view that Americans tend to be more interested (by a margin of two to one) in news about their local community than in news of the world. Black Americans (56%) are more likely than whites (40%) to say that foreign policy has a "major impact" on their lives, a tendency that is especially pronounced among college-educated blacks (64% say major impact, compared to 34% of college-educated whites).

As a first measure of foreign policy attitudes, respondents were asked to evaluate the conduct of foreign policy by all post–World War II presidents, from Harry Truman to Bill Clinton. In general, as table 3.2 shows, blacks and whites alike gave each of the presidents high marks, although there are some interesting, apparently partisan-based, race differences. There are significant gaps and gulfs between blacks and whites in the evaluation of Johnson, Nixon, Reagan, and Clinton. Blacks were much less likely to view the foreign policy records of Nixon and Reagan as successful, although both these presidents, arguably, had quite good records, including Nixon's détente with the Soviet Union, several arms control agreements with the Soviets, and his diplomatic opening to China; and under Reagan the beginnings of the collapse of the Soviet Union and the end of the Cold War. By contrast, blacks gave Johnson and Clinton relatively high evaluations despite Clinton's modest achievements and Johnson's disastrous war

Table 3.2   Racial Differences in Perceptions of the Foreign Policy Records of Postwar U.S. Presidents (% Saying President Successful)*

	Blacks	*Whites*	*Gap*	*Gulf*
Truman	88%	91%	—	
Eisenhower	87	89	—	
Kennedy	95	86	—	
Johnson	77	44		33
Nixon	57	77		20
Ford	56	53	—	
Carter	73	63	10	
Reagan	51	74		23
Bush	71	79	—	
Clinton	80	53		27

Source: Chicago Council on Foreign Relations, American Foreign Policy and Public Opinion, 1994.

*The question read: Do you feel that the following U.S. presidents have been very successful, somewhat successful, or very unsuccessful in the conduct of foreign policy? Responses include very successful and successful.

in Vietnam. Respondents here are likely reacting not to the specific foreign policy records of the presidents but rather to an overall partisan and policy identification with a president. Blacks and whites alike almost universally evaluated as successful the foreign policy records of Truman, Eisenhower, and Kennedy (near 90% in all three cases), while also sharing a consensus that Gerald Ford was the least successful in foreign policy of the ten presidents since the end of World War II.

Although interesting, the opinions on postwar presidents do not provide much insight into respondents' evaluation of the substantive foreign policies pursued by these presidents.[3] The data in table 3.3 do provide some insights into foreign policy attitudes—they reflect responses regarding whether the United States has a "vital interest" in certain countries or areas of the world, specifically, whether the countries are important to the United States for "political, economic, or security reasons." (Frequently, when used by U.S. foreign policy elites, the term "vital interests" suggests that the interests in the country or area are worth going to war for.) In general, African Americans are much less likely than whites are to see a country as vital to U.S. interests. Japan, for both blacks and whites, is clearly the most vital of nations in terms of respondents' perceptions of U.S. interests.[4] Of the nine selected countries, Brazil is the only one that blacks are more likely than whites to define as vital to U.S. interests (47% to 29%). Brazil, of course, has a large black population; but Egypt, an African country and one that is frequently valorized in Afro-centric black-nationalist circles, is nevertheless viewed as more vital by whites than blacks, 58% to 31%.

Table 3.3   Racial Differences in Perceptions of Countries "Vital" to U.S. Interests (% Saying Country Is Vital to U.S. Interest)*

	Blacks	Whites	Gap	Gulf
Egypt	31%	58%		27
Germany	48	78		30
Japan	80	91	11	
Mexico	61	85		24
Israel	56	77		21
Canada	51	81		30
Brazil	47	29	18	
Russia	65	88		23
Ukraine	32	47	15	

Source: Chicago Council on Foreign Relations, American Foreign Policy and Public Opinion, 1994.

*Respondents were read a list of countries and were asked whether the United States had a "vital interest," that is, whether the country was important to the United States for political, economic, or security reasons.

Table 3.4   Racial Differences in Attitudes toward Selected Countries (% Having Positive Attitude)*

	Blacks	Whites	Gap	Gulf
Russia	29%	46%	17	
North Korea	23	8	15	
Germany	27	52		25
Mexico	37	50	13	
Iraq	25	5		20
Canada	58	79		21

Source: Chicago Council on Foreign Relations, American Foreign Policy and Public Opinion, 1994.

*Respondents were asked to rate the countries on a "feeling thermometer"—a temperature of 50 equals neutral, higher than 50 equals warm, and below 50 equals cool. Warm feelings are presented here as positive.

The data in table 3.4 show whether respondents have negative or positive attitudes toward selected countries. The differences here are modest, but there is a gulf of 25 between blacks and whites in positive attitudes toward Germany and a gulf of 21 regarding Canada (with whites more positive toward these two countries). Also, whereas hardly any whites are positive toward Iraq, 25% of blacks are (a gulf of 20), this in spite of the consistently hostile propaganda directed toward Iraq by political and media elites since the end of the Gulf War. The gap of 15 toward North Korea is also worthy of note because it is also a target of negative propaganda—a so-called "rogue nation"—but is still viewed favorably by nearly a quarter of blacks (only 8% of whites).

The purpose of this overview of racial differences in foreign policy is to provide some context for our analysis of how blacks and whites evaluated the Persian Gulf War. Related to this purpose specifically is whether there is a general predisposition on the part of Americans to use force in international affairs. Table

Table 3.5   Racial Differences in Opinion on the Use of U.S. Troops in Hypothetical Situations of Conflict (% Favoring Use of U.S. Troops)

	Blacks	Whites	Gap	Gulf
North Korea invades South Korea	25%	41%	16	
Iraq invades Saudi Arabia	39	53	14	
Arabs invade Israel	27	44	17	
Russia invades Poland	19	34	15	
Russia invades Western Europe	33	56		23
Civil War in South Africa	38	16		22

Source: Chicago Council on Foreign Relations, American Foreign Policy and Public Opinion, 1994.

3.5 shows data on respondents' views on the use of force in a series of hypothetical situations: a North Korean invasion of South Korea, Iraq invading Saudi Arabia,
an invasion of Israel by the Arab states, a Russian invasion of either Poland or
Western Europe, and the outbreak of civil war in South Africa.

Among all Americans there is a reluctance to use force in most situations,
although in each of the hypotheticals (except South Africa) black opinion is
more "dovish," or less inclined toward the use of force. In no situation is there a
black majority for the use of force—not even South Africa—whereas majorities
or near majorities of whites would go to war in the case of an Iraqi invasion of
Saudi Arabia, a Russian invasion of Western Europe, and an Arab invasion of
Israel.[5]

Although white Americans are divided and skeptical about the use of the
American military in situations of war, and blacks even more so, both blacks and
whites favor, with modest differences, the United States taking an active role in
world affairs—70% of whites and 63% of blacks. There are differences between
blacks and whites on the goals or purposes of this activism, with blacks somewhat more likely to favor a focus on human rights and helping the poor nations
of the world, although both groups overwhelmingly favor preventing the spread
of nuclear weapons as a foreign policy goal (see table 3.6).

We conclude this overview with an examination of two issues under active
policy debate at the time of CCFR's 1994 survey: (1) NATO expansion and (2)
the creation of a Palestinian state in that part of Palestine occupied by Israel. As
table 3.7 indicates, there are only modest differences on NATO expansion (to
include Poland, Hungary, and the Czech Republic). Pluralities of blacks and whites
favor expansion, but a substantial number of respondents indicated they did not
know or have an opinion. A similar pattern is observed on the question of Palestine—modest pluralities in favor but a larger segment of the population, black

Table 3.6   Racial Differences in Opinion on Foreign Policy Goals of the United States
(% Saying Goals Very Important)*

	Blacks	Whites	Gap
Improving standard of living/less-developed countries	38%	20%	18
Defending human rights	45	33	12
Preventing spread of nuclear weapons	85	74	11
Combating world hunger	65	55	10

Source: Chicago Council on Foreign Relations, American Foreign Policy and Public Opinion, 1994.

* The question read: I am going to read a list of possible foreign policy goals the United States might
have. For each one, please say whether you think it should be a very important foreign policy goal of
the United States, a somewhat important foreign policy, or not important goal at all.

Table 3.7   Racial Differences in Opinion toward NATO Expansion, a Palestinian State, and Diplomatic Recognition of Selected Countries

	Favor	*Oppose*	*Don't Know*
NATO Expansion			
Blacks	38	26	36
Whites	42	33	25
Palestinian State			
Blacks	32	22	46
Whites	39	20	41
Diplomatic Recognition *Blacks*			
North Korea	51	27	21
Vietnam	54	29	17
Cuba	54	33	14
Iran	46	42	16
Whites			
North Korea	50	39	12
Vietnam	58	32	10
Cuba	45	47	9
Iran	36	54	11

Source: Chicago Council on Foreign Relations, American Foreign Policy and Public Opinion, 1994.

and white, expressing no opinion. The response on NATO expansion is not especially surprising because at the time of the survey the issue had not been widely debated in Congress or discussed in the media.[6] The idea of an Arab state in part of Palestine has long been the subject of elite policy debate and controversy in the media, with leading African Americans (including Jesse Jackson) long favoring the idea. It is therefore somewhat surprising that most Americans do not have an opinion and that of those who do whites are a bit more in favor than blacks. Finally, the table shows only modest differences between blacks and whites on diplomatic recognition of Cuba, Vietnam, Iran, and North Korea.

For the most part, on foreign policy issues, the differences between blacks and whites are not as large as those on domestic issues—more gaps than gulfs or chasms.[7] Whites were more likely than blacks to identify various countries as vital to U.S. interests and to support the use of military force in various parts of the world (the only exception is South Africa, where blacks more so than whites would favor intervention in the event of civil war). And although a majority of blacks have negative attitudes toward North Korea and Iraq—countries defined as post–Cold War enemies, "rogue nations," in the language of the foreign policy establishment—they are less negative or hostile than whites.

Americans are divided on the use of force abroad. Just a little more than half of the white public would favor the use of force in the case of a Russian invasion of Western Europe or an Iraqi invasion of Saudi Arabia. By contrast, almost two-thirds of blacks would oppose the use of force in these situations. Yet, as the following analysis of opinion on the Gulf War will show, public opinion is highly volatile on issues of war and peace and easily manipulated—"framed" by media and political elites.

THE PERSIAN GULF WAR

Most Americans on most issues of public policy most of the time do not have an opinion (Kinder, 1983; Sniderman, 1993). Rather, their responses to questions in polls and surveys are shaped by the wording and sequencing of questions, by the context of the public debate at the time of the survey, and even by such idiosyncratic considerations as the mood of the respondent at the time of the interview. This phenomenon is especially evident when the question deals with unfamiliar issues of foreign policy in distant "foreign" countries. This was certainty the case with opinion on the Persian Gulf War, which changed dramatically from survey to survey and sometimes within the same survey.

One way to deal with opinion volatility is to analyze a number of surveys or polls on a particular issue over an extended period of time. This procedure allows the analyst to some extent to determine the basic underlying shape of public opinion, as well as to see how it is framed by public debate and events. For three of the controversies examined in this book—O. J. Simpson, Marion Barry, and the Persian Gulf War—we have numerous surveys over the period of nearly a year or more, which allows us to sort out the fundamentals of opinion in a dynamic, contextual analysis.

The *Washington Post* and ABC News conducted twelve polls during the course of the Gulf War, from the Iraqi invasion in August 1990 to February 1991 when the war ended (see table 3.8 for a time line of major events during the war). The polls asked about several issues, including whether the United States would win the war, the expected casualties, the use of nuclear weapons, the killing of Iraqi leader Saddam Hussein, and President Bush's overall handling of the crisis. We focus primarily on questions dealing with support for the president's decision to send troops to the Gulf and support for the use of the military to force Iraqi withdrawal.

Table 3.8   Time Line of Persian Gulf War, Selected Major Events, August 1990–April 1991

August 2	Iraq invades Kuwait.
August 3	UN condemns invasion.
August 6	Bush demands complete withdrawal.
August 9	Iraq annexes Kuwait.
August 10	United States imposes economic blockade.
August 17	Thousands of U.S. troops sent to Saudi Arabia.
September 26	UN imposes economic blockade.
October 18	Senate Foreign Relations Committee demands congressional approval prior to war.
October 25	Congressional leaders reserve right to approve decision to go to war.
November 6	Democrats gain seats in midterm congressional elections.
November 8	Bush sends more than 150,000 troops to Persiain Gulf to prepare for "offensive option."
November 15	Bush assures Congress he will consult before war.
December 5	House Democrats urge no war before approval of Congress.
December 15	Congressional leaders visit Persian Gulf.
January 4	Congress reconvenes.
January 15	Congress approves war, 52–47 in Senate, 250–183 in House.
January 17	United States begins air war over Iraq.
January 18	Iraq launches missile attack on Israel.
February 21	Ground war begins.
February 23	Bush ends war, declares "Kuwait is liberated."
April 1	U.S. army begins withdrawing.

PHASES IN THE GULF WAR AND THE DYNAMICS OF PUBLIC OPINION

The Gulf crisis may be divided into four phases: (1) the Iraqi invasion of Kuwait and the initial American response, (2) the buildup to the decision to go to war, (3) the war itself, and (4) its immediate aftermath.

Phase I: Iraq Invades Kuwait

Iraq invaded Kuwait on August 2, 1990. On August 17, thousands of American troops were dispatched to neighboring Saudi Arabia, in anticipation of a possible Iraqi attack. The *Washington Post* first asked respondents if they favored or opposed Bush's decision to send troops to the Persian Gulf: 77% of whites and 40% of blacks favored the decision. Thus, at the outset of the crisis, there was a gulf of 37 in opinion between blacks and whites. As table 3.9 indicates, there were also race-gender effects on opinion, with white men the strongest supporters of the decision, black women the strongest opponents. In general, women were more

Table 3.9   Race–Gender Differences in Opinion toward the Initial Bush Administration Response to the Iraqi Invasion of Kuwait

% Supporting Bush Decision to Send Troops to Persian Gulf				Gap	Gulf
Blacks	40%	Whites	77%		37
Men	52	Men	89		37
Women	31	Women	61		30

% Favoring U.S. Invasion to Force Iraqi Withdrawal					
Blacks	29	Whites	28		—
Men	40	Men	30	10	
Women	19	Women	25		—

% Favoring U.S. Taking All Action, Including Military Power to Force Iraqi Withdrawal					
Blacks	68	Whites	60		—
Men	69	Men	71		—
Women	53	Women	63	10	

Source: *Washington Post*/ABC News, August 1990.

likely to be opposed to the decision, but the gender difference was a gap, the race difference a chasm.

This first *Post* survey asked respondents whether the United States should invade Kuwait to force Iraqi withdrawal (the question was framed by noting that Iraq had a million troops, 5,000 tanks, and 500 combat aircraft). Surprisingly, there was no race difference—29% of whites and 28% of blacks favored an American invasion. Yet, later in this same poll, when respondents were asked to agree or disagree with the statement "The U.S. should take all action, including the use of military force to make Iraq withdraw," opinion almost reversed itself—68% of blacks and 60% of whites agreed (the racial difference here is not statistically significant). This points to the importance of question wording in shaping opinion. Although a majority of blacks were opposed to the decision to send troops to the Gulf, in this same poll, they indicated support for the use of those troops to effectuate Iraqi withdrawal.

A second *Washington Post* poll conducted later in August found that 75% of both blacks and whites agreed that it was "very important" that Iraq withdraw from Kuwait. Yet, a large race gulf of 31 remained between the races on Bush's decision to send troops to the region—85% of whites approved but only 54% of blacks. However, this race gulf virtually disappeared when respondents were asked to agree or disagree that the United States "should take all actions, including the use of force" to make Iraq withdraw—80% of blacks agreed and 70% of whites.

This question was number 11 in the poll, but on number 15, when respondents were asked whether the United States should invade, only 50% of whites and 42% of blacks agreed.

Clearly at the outset of the crisis, opinion was muddled and inconsistent. In this second poll, respondents were also asked whether they thought U.S. involvement in the Persian Gulf conflict was for upholding the principle of not allowing one country to invade another or for "economics and oil," that is, for moral or economic reasons. Both blacks and whites saw U.S. involvement in the Gulf as based on oil and economics rather than on moral principles; but there was a modest gap of 19—82% of blacks, but 63% of whites.

Phase II: The Buildup to War

The third *Post* poll was conducted in November 1990. Between the August 1990 polls and this November poll, a number of critical events had occurred: Bush had declared that the Iraqi invasion "would not stand"; the United Nations condemned the invasion and called for Iraqi withdrawal; the United States and its allies (with UN authorization) had imposed an economic blockade on Iraq; and meanwhile, Iraq had formally annexed Kuwait.

At home the president and Congress were involved in a crisis of sorts involving the budget, resulting in a one-day shutdown of the government. And, as Congress approached adjournment for the fall election, the Senate Foreign Relations Committee passed a resolution demanding that President Bush get congressional approval prior to any military action in the Gulf. The Speaker of the House and the Majority Leader of the Senate indicated that they might reconvene Congress after the election if it appeared Bush was prepared to go to war.

Immediately after the congressional elections (in which the President's party lost seats), the president called up thousands of combat reserve troops and announced he was sending up to 350,000 troops to the Gulf in order to provide an "adequate military option" for war. Leaders of Congress once again called for the convening of a special session of Congress. Bush rejected this call, but he indicated he would "consult" Congress before taking offensive military action. Also in November, the U.N. Security Council approved a resolution authorizing the use of force to expel Iraq from Kuwait after a January 15 deadline. It is in this context of presidential–congressional conflict over the prospects of impending war that this November poll was conducted.

There was a racial gulf of 35 in approval of Bush's handling of the crisis— 61% of whites approved but only 26% of blacks (college-educated blacks were somewhat less likely to approve and black women, only 15%, were significantly less likely to approve). Yet when asked later in this same poll whether the United States should take all action necessary to secure Iraqi withdrawal, there is only a modest gap of 12 (whites 70%, black 58%). This represents hardly any change from the prebuildup August polls. Whites were more likely (76% to 52%) to approve the UN resolution on the use of force, and 51% of blacks compared to 68% of whites approved of going to war after the January 15 deadline, a modest gap of 17.

Responses indicated a closing of the race chasm and evolving consensus in support of war. However, on the part of blacks, this support is ambivalent. Seventy-seven percent of whites and 72% of blacks at this time were convinced that the United States would in fact go to war. But when asked, "All in all, do you approve of sending troops or should we have stayed out?" the gulf (32) in opinion returned—72% of whites approved of sending troops but only 40% of blacks. There were especially strong race-gender effects on this question—88% of white men approved, 73% of black men, 63% of white women, but only 19% of black women. Throughout the conflict, black women remained most skeptical about the war.

The fourth *Post* poll was conducted on January 13, 1991, two days before the January 15 war deadline. The race chasm in approval of Bush's handling of the crisis is still evident at 40 (72% of whites, 32% of blacks). However, on the approval of the use of force, the race difference is a more modest gulf of 24 (79% of whites, 55% of blacks. Yet several questions later, the chasm reappears—78% of whites but only 37% of blacks agreed that the U.S. should go to war after January 15. Blacks also were more likely to favor talks with Iraq prior to going to war (76% to 55%) and to believe (62% to 33%) that such talks could avoid war.

After an emotional debate in Congress, the Senate by a narrow margin (52 to 47) and the House by a larger margin (250 to 183) passed a resolution approving an attack on Iraq after January 15. Eighty-one percent of whites approved of the resolution, but only 47% of blacks, a gulf of 34.

Thus, as the war approached, white America and its leaders had reached a consensus on the war option. Although black opinion was ambivalent and contradictory, in general it stood apart from this consensus. Less than a majority of blacks approved of the congressional war resolution, compared to 81% of whites. And while white members of Congress were divided on the war resolution, with one exception—the lone black House Republican—the entire twenty-six-person black congressional delegation voted no. In the African American community, there was already an emergent antiwar movement led by such people as Jesse Jackson and Coretta Scott King, the widow of Dr. Martin Luther King Jr. (Duke, 1991).

Phase III: The War

After the war started, the *Post* and ABC News conducted a series of tracking or "pulse" polls, which measured the response of the public to the war as it unfolded. The results of these polls are reported in table 3.10. The first of these polls was

Table 3.10 Racial Differences in Approval of the War, January 18–February 27, 1991*

	Blacks	Whites	Gulf	Chasm
January 18	37%	66%	29	
February 18	30	66	36	
February 22	24	66		42
February 24	57	87	30	
February 27	36	74	38	

Source: *Washington Post*/ABC News.

*The number of blacks in these pulse polls samples was very small, from 36 to 50. Thus, the results here should be interpreted cautiously.

conducted on January 18, 1991, three days after the air attack on Iraq began. Approval of the war then deeply divided the country across the color line—66% of whites strongly approved, but only 37% of blacks (a gulf of 29).

As soon as the war started, a nascent antiwar, or protest, movement emerged. This movement was strongly supported by the African American leadership community; however, the movement was small and isolated, and it received relatively little media attention. Approval of the antiwar protests was indeed stronger among blacks (51%) than whites (27%). Approval of Bush also reflected a racial gulf (36)—66% of whites and 30% of blacks. This approval of the antiwar protests and disapproval of President Bush reflected the continued black skepticism about the war. In the war's first week, only 26% of blacks approved of the decision to go to war, compared to 56% of whites, a gulf of 30.[8]

The second tracking poll was conducted a month later on February 18. Once again there was a large gulf, a near chasm, of 36 in approval of the war—30% of blacks, 66% of whites. Respondents were also asked whether they would approve of going to a ground war if the now monthlong air war failed to win Iraqi withdrawal. Again blacks were ambivalent about the war—only 29% approved of the decision to go war, but 65% favored a ground war if necessary. There was still a race gulf of 16 (81% of whites favored a ground war if the air war failed). This again shows the importance of context and question wording because among both blacks and whites there is apparently an increase in approval for ground combat among persons who oppose the war.

Three more polls were conducted prior to the war's end. The February 22 poll again found the persistent race difference in "strong approval" of the war decision. Indeed, the race gulf had become a chasm of 42—66% of whites strongly approved, but only 24% of blacks. In this poll respondents were also asked whether the United States should talk with Iraq to avoid the ground war; 79% of blacks favored diplomacy, but only 44% of whites, a gulf of 35.

A February 24 poll found the consistent race gulf in approval of the war. In this poll respondents were also asked, "In view of recent developments, was the war a mistake?" Here the race difference became a modest gap—18% of whites and 28% of blacks said that the war was a mistake. In this same poll, only 57% of blacks expressed approval of the war (87% of whites); thus the response on whether the war was a mistake reflected the consistent black ambivalence about the war. This ambivalence was also seen in how blacks and whites responded to a question about how to respond if Iraq used chemical weapons, specifically, whether the United States should respond in kind or use only "conventional weapons." A conventional response was favored by 49% of whites but only 22% of blacks. This race gulf of 27 was surprising given overall black "dovishness" on the war.

The final pulse poll was conducted on February 27, the day after Iraqi troops retreated across the border and American troops entered Kuwait city. Again, even as victory became apparent, there was a wide gulf (38) in approval of the war decision—74% among whites, 36% among blacks. Although the races differed on approval of the war, there was no race difference on the goals of the war in terms of forcing Iraq to withdraw from Kuwait rather than ousting Saddam Hussein (which some policy elites and media commentators proposed). Twenty-four percent of whites and 18% of blacks favored attempting to kill the Iraqi leader, and 95% of whites and 87% of blacks favored putting the Iraqi head of state on trial for war crimes.

Phase IV: The War Ends

The final *Post* poll on the Gulf War was conducted in March 1991, after the February 28 cease-fire. John F. Kennedy remarked after the failure of the American-sponsored invasion of Cuba at the Bay of Pigs that "victory has a thousand fathers, defeat is an orphan." The reaction of the public (and virtually all political leaders and commentators) to the U.S. victory in the Gulf War demonstrated the truth of Kennedy's quip.

The Persian Gulf War has been described as "a war that fits closely that old, romantic image—clean, successful, largely painless, exciting, and suffused with good feelings of potency and solidarity alike" (Hallin and Gitlin, 1994: 162). Although the Democratic leadership in Congress had opposed the decision to go to war in early January (preferring to wait to see if the economic sanctions and blockade would result in Iraqi withdrawal), once the war was won, virtually the entire political establishment and mainstream media joined in the victory celebration. And because it is well established that on foreign policy in general and on war in particular mass opinion tends to follow elite opinion (Mueller, 1973), it is not surprising that mass opinion joined in this elite consensus.

On January 20, 1991, three days after the start of the war, 66% of whites and 30% of blacks approved of Bush's handling of the Persian Gulf crisis. In the last *Post* poll, conducted in March 1991, 88% of blacks and 96% of whites approved of Bush's conduct in the Gulf (see table 3.11). In this period of less than three months, Bush's approval among whites increased 30% and among blacks an astonishing 58%, virtually eliminating the consistent race differences in approval of Bush's handling of the crisis. Again, the opinion change is most striking among blacks, because from the outset of the crisis blacks had been skeptical about Bush's Gulf policy.

Approval of Bush's handling of the Gulf crisis translated into an increase in approval of his overall job performance—69% among whites and 52% among blacks (a gap of 17). When asked how they would vote if the presidential election were held that day, 80% of whites and 59% of blacks indicated they would vote for Bush rather than for the Democratic candidate, a race gulf of only 21. Again, this points to the importance of the context—in this case, the "rally around the winners" phenomenon.

The last question from this March 1991 poll showed the dimension of this postvictory consensus. When asked if the war was worth fighting, 90% of whites and 72% of blacks said yes. Again, the change in black opinion was most striking. In the last *Post* pulse poll conducted when American victory seemed near, only 36% of blacks expressed approval of the war, compared to 74% of whites, a race gulf of 38. At the end of the war, this race difference was a modest 17. Although the most striking finding here is the narrowing of the race difference, it remains true that even in victory blacks remained somewhat more skeptical about the war's worthiness.

Finally, respondents were asked whether the war was fought to vindicate the moral principle that no country should invade another or whether it was fought for oil and economics. Moral principle was the reason given by 69% of whites and 51% of blacks. When this question was first asked in August 1990, 82% of blacks and 63% of whites said for oil and economics.

Table 3.11   Racial Differences in Opinion toward the War after the Cease-Fire

	Blacks	*Whites*	*Gap*	*Gulf*
Approval of Bush handling of Gulf War	88%	96%	—	
Approval of overall Bush job performance as president	69	52	17	
Would vote for Bush in 1992	59	80		21
Was war worth fighting? (% yes)	72	90	18	
Was war for economics and oil or for moral principles? (% saying moral principle)	51	69	18	

Source: *Washington Post*/ABC News, March 1991.

THE PERSIAN GULF WAR: A PERSPECTIVE ON BLACK-WHITE OPINION DIFFERENCES

At the outset of this analysis, we noted that public opinion on most issues is structured by how the issue is framed by the elites of politics and media, and that this was especially the case on foreign policy. The Persian Gulf War is a case—a textbook case—of this phenomenon (see the case studies in Bennett and Paletz, 1994). From the outset of the crisis, President Bush and the national media in what former CBS News diplomatic correspondent Marvin Kalb called "patriotic journalism" successfully framed the crisis so as to structure a favorable public opinion. Thus, Kalb wrote, "was it then any wonder that the overwhelming majority of the American people supported the war?" (Kalb, 1994: 4, 5).

In the early stages of the crisis when Bush dispatched troops to the Gulf, there was virtual unanimity in the establishment media and among national political leaders in support of the President. And throughout the subsequent debate leading up to the congressional debate, vote, and the war, "Few criticisms challenged fundamental aspects of the administration's policy. In particular, nearly all reported critics as well as supporters agreed that *Iraq must be unconditionally dislodged from Kuwait by force, if necessary*" (Entman and Page, 1994: 94–95, emphasis in original). Even Jesse Jackson, the preeminent leader of African Americans and an important leader of the left, joined this consensus. So did George McGovern, the 1960s antiwar leader and 1972 presidential nominee. The congressional and media critics of the Bush policy therefore did not challenge the war option but rather its timing—not whether war but when.

Thus, Entman and Page referred to the "intellectual narrowness of the deliberations" (1994: 95). For example, there was no real discussion of the United States alliance with Iraq in its war of several years before with Iran. No discussion—none—of the colonial creation of the oil-rich Kuwait ministate (which might have given some legitimacy to Iraq's claim on the territory). There was also not much discussion—some but not much—of the venal, authoritarian rule of Kuwait's emir and his family. And to the extent that the issue was framed around access to oil, the obvious point was rarely made: It was not likely that Iraq would cut off oil supplies to the United States or to its allies, even if it controlled the Kuwait reserves.

Not only was the debate intellectually and politically narrow, it was in some ways Orwellian. Dorman and Livingston, in analyzing the framing of the issue, wrote, "Like one of the sudden and socially unacknowledged transformation of friend to foe in Orwell's *1984*, Saddam the ally became Hitler incarnate virtually overnight" (1994: 66). The president, Republican congressional leaders, and television and newspaper commentators frequently used the Hitler-and-Nazi-Germany frame. This propaganda campaign was developed, tested, and marketed by the influential Washington public relations firm of Hill and Knowlton (Trento, 1992).

In this context, Kalb was correct: Is it any wonder that an overwhelming majority of the American people eventually supported the war?

Yet Kalb is only in part correct. It is more accurate to say that an overwhelming majority of white Americans supported the war. Although attitudes varied depending on the context and the question wording, almost from the outset, a majority of whites supported the sending of troops to the Gulf, the buildup to the war, and the war itself. Almost the exact opposite was the case for African Americans. From the beginning of the crisis until the cease-fire, there were large gaps, gulfs, and occasionally chasms in opinion on the war, with most blacks opposing the initial dispatch of troops, the buildup to the war, and the war itself. Only at war's end did majorities of blacks support the war. And even then there was a modest race gap. For example, 90% of whites said the war was worth fighting, but only 73% of blacks.

What these race differences in opinion on the war tended to show was that most black Americans apparently ignored mainstream, establishment framing of the issue and/or employed alternative frames. There was little fundamental elite opposition to U.S. war aims that might have structured black opinion, and the war's military commander and spokesman at home was an articulate and poised African American, Joint Chiefs Chair Colin Powell. Yet black opinion remained skeptical.

Historically, African Americans have been skeptical about America's foreign wars, especially in the so-called Third World. From the Mexican American War to the war in Vietnam, African American leaders were in the forefront of the opposition. This may reflect to some extent African American identification with the colonial peoples of the world, who like themselves have suffered from white European exploitation and race subordination. African Americans, for example, more so than whites saw the Gulf War as having more to do with oil and economics than high moral principles.

Finally, 25% of the troops serving in the Gulf were black (including 30% of the army ground troops and 50% of the female troops). Thus, African Americans may have been concerned about the prospects of disproportionately high black casualties in a prolonged conflict. As it turned out, the war was short and relatively costless in terms of injuries and deaths to Americans (about a hundred casualties in the brief ground war). Therefore, despite skepticism, this may have made the war seem worthwhile; and thus blacks were able to join in the victory celebration.

HAITI

African Americans have long had an interest in Haiti, the first black republic (established in 1804) and the first case of a successful black revolution against white colonial domination. The United States has had an ambivalent relationship with Haiti and was the last of the Western nations to open normal diplomatic relations with the country (during the administration of Abraham Lincoln). For much of Haiti's history, the United States has dominated this small country's economic and political life, placing the country under military rule from 1917 to 1934 (Wienstein, 1992). Throughout this long period of U.S. domination, African American leaders protested; but in effect "Haiti had already become, for all practical purposes, a part of America's Negro empire" (Franklin, 1967: 430).

From the end of the American occupation until 1991, Haiti was for the most part governed by the corrupt and brutal Duvaliers, a father-and-son dictatorship ("Papa Doc" and "Baby Doc") that was supported by the United States. When the United States finally forced Baby Doc into exile, the people of Haiti chose Jean Bertrand Aristide as president in a historic free and democratic election in 1991. However, after less than eight months in office, Aristide was ousted in a military coup led by General Raoul Cedras.

In order to suppress popular support for Aristide (who was exiled in the United States), the military regime began to brutalize and terrorize the Haitian people, which in turn led thousands to flee to the United States in dangerous and unsafe boats. The Bush administration refused to admit the Haitians, claiming they were leaving Haiti for economic rather than political reasons and, therefore, were not eligible for political asylum. While running for president in 1992, Clinton criticized Bush's policy regarding the Haitian refugees, calling it illegal and immoral. However, once in office Clinton continued the Bush policy, which resulted in strong protests by African American leaders. Randall Robinson, the head of TransAfrica, even engaged in a hunger strike to protest Clinton policy (see Fullwood, 1993; Holmes, 1994).

Some African American leaders called on the Clinton administration to use the military to force the ouster of the military regime and to restore Aristide to power. The United Nations had imposed sanctions on the Haitian regime, but they apparently were not working. So many black leaders called for the use of military force to remove the Cedras military dictatorship.

The Haitian crisis thus provides an interesting subtext to opinion differences of blacks and whites on the U.S. role in international affairs and the use of force abroad. In general, as we have seen, blacks more so than whites are less likely to see any country as vital to U.S. interests and much less likely to favor the use of force in international affairs. How are these attitudes affected when the country is the oldest black republic in the world and when those calling for the use of force are prominent African Americans? Specifically, we expect bonds of racial solidarity to come into play here in shaping the opinions of blacks.

In table 3.12, data are reported from a May 1994 *Washington Post*/ABC News poll on attitudes toward the Haitian situation. Most Americans did not think Haiti was in the "vital interests" of the United States; however, half of blacks did, com-

Table 3.12   Racial Difference in Opinion on the Haitian Crisis

	Blacks	*White*	*Gap*	*Gulf*
Haiti in vital interest of United States? (% yes)	50%	33%	17	
Are Haitians fleeing their country for economic reasons or for fear of political persecution? (% saying persecution)	35	15		20
Should United States turn back Haitian refugees? (% yes)	43	71		28
Should Haitians be interviewed before returned in order to determine status or simply turned backed (% should be interviewed)	89	61		28
United States, if necessary, should use military force to restore democratic government to Haiti. (% favoring use of force)	48	36	12	

Source: *Washington Post*/ABC News, May 1994.

pared to one-third of whites. This gap of 17 is almost certainly a function or an expression of racial solidarity with the black republic, given the context that Haiti is the only nation for which blacks more so than whites see a U.S. vital interest. This sense of international racial solidarity is also displayed in the other questions in the poll, which dealt with treatment of the Haitian refugees and the use of force to oust the military regime.

African Americans were more likely to agree that the Haitians were leaving their country because of political persecution rather than poverty (gulf of 20); that the refugee boats should not be turned back (gulf of 28); and that before any refugees were sent back they should be interviewed in order to admit those who in fact could prove political persecution. (It was the policy of the Clinton administration to return would-be refugees without interviews or hearings.) Finally, nearly half of blacks (compared to a third of whites) favored the use of force to oust the military regime and restore the elected president, but this is a gap of only 12, indicating even here that black opinion is relatively dovish.[9]

However, African Americans' foreign policy opinions, like those of Jews, Greeks, Poles, and Italians, are shaped by a sense of ethnic or racial kinship (Deconde, 1992). Similar racial differences in opinion structured the opinions of blacks and whites about the U.S. policy toward South Africa (Fierce, 1982).

BLACKS AND FOREIGN POLICY: AN AFRO-CENTRIC PERSPECTIVE

Although race differences in opinion on foreign policy are not as large as on domestic issues, there are nevertheless race gaps and gulfs. African American opinion on foreign policy and on the use of force abroad tends to be somewhat more dovish than white opinion. Blacks are less likely to see any country (except

Haiti!) as vital to U.S. interests; and for no country were majorities of blacks willing to support the use of force to repel a hypothetical invasion. This was vividly shown during the Persian Gulf War. Although white opinion was initially skeptical about Bush's decision to go to war in the Persian Gulf, early on it stabilized around two-thirds support. By contrast, blacks' opinion, although ambivalent and sometimes contradictory, remained mainly opposed until the war's end, when they too joined in the national consensus around the quick and easy victory.

Black mass opposition to the Gulf War is all the more remarkable because there was little elite or media opposition and because, in general, public opinion on foreign policy and war opinion tends to follow closely elite opinion.[10] A divided elite tends to cue a divided public. This appears not to be the case for black opinion. Although the black congressional delegation was nearly unanimous in its opposition to the war resolution and, after the war started, Jesse Jackson and others joined a nascent antiwar movement, these events were not widely publicized either in the mainstream media or in the weekly black press.

So why didn't blacks support the war? We are inclined to believe that ambivalent opposition is rooted in historical and structural forces that allow the black community to resist, more so than whites, mainstream, elite framing of foreign policy issues.[11] Historically, from the Mexican American War to the Vietnam War, blacks have tended to oppose American wars in general and those wars in the Third World in particular. This latter tendency represents a kind of Third World solidarity with people of color; what one scholar referred to more broadly as an Afro-Centric perspective (Henderson, 1995).

Structurally, given their disproportionate representation in the American armed forces (especially its combat units), blacks know they will bear disproportionate casualties. Many blacks feel that racism and inequality force many young black women and men to enter the armed forces. As Congresswoman Maxine Waters of South Central Los Angeles said during the Gulf War, "It's not fair. Something is wrong. It's not fair for me to be made to volunteer [for the military] to be educated, to get trained, to have a job, to have a roof over my head. Something is wrong in an America that does not provide me an opportunity for a better quality of life" (quoted in Duke, 1991). Even the relatively conservative National Urban League issued a statement at the start of the Gulf War saying, "We urge a nation willing to go to war for its principles to make an equivalent effort to end the inequality that subverts those same principles at home" (quoted in Duke, 1991).[12]

Finally, many blacks see hypocrisy not only at home, as the Urban League statement implies, but also abroad in the conduct of foreign policy, that is, a nation more concerned about democracy in Poland than in South Africa or in Cuba more than in Haiti.[13] Thus, blacks were more likely to view the Gulf War as more about oil and economics than about principles and morality. This overall tendency is reflected in the fact that blacks tend to be less hostile to those nations defined by U.S. elites as "rogue nations," such as Cuba and Iran.

These historical and structural factors provide black Americans with a different perspective from which to frame issues of foreign policy and war.

NOTES

1. The standard source on U.S. foreign policy and African Americans is Miller (1978). Useful material is also in Deconde's (1992) study of broader ethnic influences on foreign policy. See also Skinner (1992), Stanford (1997), and Walton and Smith (2000: chap. 16).

2. Unfortunately, the sample sizes in several of these surveys are very small, resulting in some black subsamples of less than forty. The results, therefore, must be read with caution.

3. An indicator of the shifting, partisan, and largely uninformed character of public evaluation of presidential foreign policy performance, in its 1998 survey, the CCFR found that President Clinton ranked first among U.S. presidents on foreign policy, up from eighth in the 1994 survey. This evaluation of Clinton is probably a reflection of his overall high approval rating in the polls at the time of the survey because he had no noteworthy foreign policy successes at the time of the 1998 survey (Associated Press, 1999a).

4. In general, college-educated blacks are more likely to see countries as vital to U.S. interests. For example, 66% of college-educated blacks see Germany as vital, and 73% see Mexico as vital.

5. There were no significant education differences, but black women were especially skeptical about going to war to defend any country.

6. After a lackluster debate and little attention by the media, the Senate in the spring of 1998 approved the expansion of NATO to include the three countries.

7. The largest difference in foreign policy opinions between blacks and whites involved not countries or issues but leadership. Respondents were asked to evaluate several world leaders (Iraqi President Saddam Hussein, German Chancellor Helmut Kohl, and President Clinton, among others), including South African President Nelson Mandela. Eighty-two percent of blacks indicated positive feelings toward Mandela but only 44% of whites, a gulf of 38. This gulf was larger than for any world leader, as well as for any other foreign policy issue.

8. Throughout the war and afterward, there was a debate in the press and among policy elites about whether the United States should attempt to kill the Iraqi leader. In the January 18 poll, 49% of whites and 53% of blacks said yes. However, a gulf of 29 divided the races in terms of whether military actions should be avoided if civilians might be killed in the process—66% of blacks said yes, compared to 37% of whites.

9. The crisis in Haiti was finally resolved when President Clinton sent former President Jimmy Carter, General Colin Powell, and Senator Sam Nunn to negotiate a settlement. Under threat of an imminent U.S. invasion, the Haitian military leaders agreed to leave and allow Aristide to return as president.

10. There were fairly strong and consistent class differences in opposition to the Gulf War. Lower-class blacks (those with only a high school education) were more likely to

favor the war than were middle-class, college-educated blacks. This finding occurred on a variety of questions throughout the various phases of the war.

11. The divisions on the war appear to have been more than black-white. In one of the few polls that sampled Latino opinion, the *Los Angeles Times* in late January 1991 found that 66% of Latinos supported the decision to go to war, compared to 88% of whites and 48% of blacks (see Duke, 1991).

12. Several critics of the war noted that Bush vetoed the Civil Rights Act of 1990 in the same month as the Iraqi invasion.

13. The black political establishment supported the invasion of Haiti in order to restore the democratically elected government; however, it has been usefully argued that "the Clinton political objective in restoring Aristide to power reflected less a universal commitment to democracy than an effort to create a permeable democracy in which restructured state institutions (especially the military and police) and an economic development model (free markets) would serve long-term U.S. interests in Haiti, as well as those of the country's international creditors and, to a lesser extent, the privileged local elite." This is why, these authors argue, the United States rejected Aristide's plea to abolish the military, to prosecute the officers for human rights abuses, and to disarm the paramilitaries (see Morley and McGillion, 1997).

4

Blacks Leading America and Leading African Americans: Louis Farrakhan, Colin Powell, and Clarence Thomas, with Reference to the Anita Hill Controversy

This chapter focuses on leadership. Lane and Sears (1964: 2–3) reminded us that the "something" public opinion may be about is, among other things, choice and preference in leadership. We examine how blacks and whites evaluate three well-known African Americans who play or have played national leadership roles. These three people represent divergent ideological and institutional roles in the leadership of the United States and of the African American community. Two have been and are controversial figures in national politics, while the third is less so.

The first leader on whom we sample opinion is Louis Farrakhan, frequently referred to as the "controversial" leader of the Nation of Islam, the most influential black nationalist organization in the United States. The second is General Colin Powell, National Security Adviser under President Reagan and Chair of the Joint Chiefs of Staff under President Bush. Finally, we look at opinion about Supreme Court Justice Clarence Thomas in general and in the context of the controversy generated by charges of sexual harassment by his former employee, Anita Hill. Three leaders—a radical black nationalist, a mainstream, establishment leader, and an outspoken black conservative—provide interesting case studies in racial differences in opinion. Frequently, studies in race opinion focus on issues, ideas, and ideology about race, racism, and inequality. These studies in leadership provide another angle, another insight into the dynamics of race and public opinion.

For opinion on Minister Farrakhan, we examined two national surveys, the first conducted by *New York Times*/CBS News in February 1994. The second was conducted in October 1995 by *Time*/CNN News, shortly after the Million Man March, which Farrakhan led in Washington, D.C. These two surveys allow us to see how opinion is shaped by the context of a major event. Similarly, we have three surveys on Justice Thomas, which also allow for dynamic contextual analysis.

LOUIS FARRAKHAN

For more than thirty years, Louis Farrakhan has been an important and influential leader in the African American community. However, it was not until Jesse Jackson's 1984 presidential campaign that he became widely known to the American public, the white public especially.[1] Farrakhan's leadership role in black America derives from his position as a leading minister in the Nation of Islam (popularly known as the Black Muslims), the proto-Islamic black nationalist organization formed by Elijah Muhammad in the 1930s (Lincoln, 1961; Clegg, 1997). By the late 1960s the Nation of Islam had become the largest black nationalist organization since Marcus Garvey's Universal Negro Improvement Association of the 1920s. And except for Malcolm X and Elijah Muhammad, Farrakhan was the best-known leader of the Nation during the 1960s and 1970s. He had inherited Malcolm X's Harlem Mosque (the most influential mosque outside of the Chicago headquarters) and Malcolm's title as national spokesman.

When Elijah Muhammad died in 1976, he was succeeded by his son Wallace Muhammad. Although Elijah had designated Wallace as his successor, almost immediately Wallace began to repudiate the core principles of black nationalism in the Nation's ideology and to move the organization away from its proto-Islam stance toward orthodox Islam. As a result, within a year, the Nation of Islam was no more. It had been thoroughly Americanized as a mainstream, orthodox religious institution.

When Wallace Muhammad inaugurated his radical changes in the Nation,

Farrakhan was dissatisfied but largely remained publicly silent. He traveled abroad in Africa and the Islamic world. On returning to the United States, he decided he could no longer accept the Nation's transformation and thus publicly broke with Wallace. He then set about to rebuild the Nation on the basis of the original principles of Elijah Muhammad.

By the early 1980s, the Nation of Islam under Farrakhan's leadership was once again flourishing. With about 120 mosques nationwide, a national newspaper, radio and television outlets, and numerous small-business enterprises, the Nation is once again the most important black nationalist organization in the United States and one of several of the most important black organizations of whatever ideology.[2]

Although Farrakhan was well known in black America (where he drew large crowds at rallies in virtually all major American cities with large black populations),[3] he was little known to the white mass public until 1984. In that year Farrakhan endorsed Jesse Jackson's candidacy for the presidency. In the course of the campaign, Farrakhan attacked a black reporter who had revealed that in private conversations Jackson sometimes referred to Jews as "Hymies" and to New York City as "Hymietown," and later Farrakhan referred to Judaism as a dirty religion. Both of these events received extensive coverage in the national press, and as a result Farrakhan became much better known. Indeed he became the second-most-recognized leader after Jesse Jackson in the black community.

In a February 1994 *New York Times*/CBS News poll dealing with race relations in general, respondents were asked two questions about Minister Farrakhan and his leadership. Table 4.1 shows data on the first question—whether people had a favorable or unfavorable opinion of Farrakhan or were undecided or did not know enough to have an opinion. The data are displayed by race, education, gender, and age. In the Race category, it is interesting that more blacks than whites declined to express an opinion; but of those with an unfavorable opinion, a massive chasm of 44 is observed—78% of whites and 34% of blacks viewed Farrakhan unfavorably. A statistically trivial 4% of whites had a favorable opinion of Farrakhan, compared to 36% of blacks—a gulf of 32. Whites are a near monolith in their opinion of Farrakhan. Among blacks, however, there is a tendency for college-educated blacks to be more favorable.

Data on the second question showed a much smaller race difference—gaps, not gulfs or chasms—in terms of whether respondents thought Farrakhan and the Nation represented the views of most blacks. About one-fourth of blacks said the minister does represent most blacks, compared to 7% of whites—a gap of 18.

Overall, although viewed more favorably by blacks than whites, Farrakhan is by no means a consensus black leader—as many blacks view him unfavorably as favorably, and only one-fourth view him as representing mainstream black America.

How did the highly successful and nationally televised Million Man March called for and led by Farrakhan affect public opinion? The march was successful in that perhaps as many as a million black men gathered on the Washington Mall.

Table 4.1   Attitudes toward Minister Louis Farrakhan by Race, Education, Gender, and Age, February 1994

	Favorable	Unfavorable	Don't Know/No Opinion
Race			
Blacks	36%	34%	30%
Whites	4	78	18
High School Ed.			
Blacks	28	38	34
Whites	5	69	25
College Ed.			
Blacks	40	32	28
Whites	3	81	16
Men			
Blacks	38	30	30
Whites	4	77	20
Women			
Blacks	33	37	34
Whites	4	80	17
18–29			
Blacks	32	34	34
Whites	3	66	32
30–44			
Blacks	38	28	34
Whites	4	77	19
45+			
Blacks	35	43	22
Whites	4	81	15

Source: *New York Times*/CBS News Poll, February 1994.

Did the march serve to enhance Farrakhan's favorability and enhance support for his leadership among blacks? Among whites? Occurring more than a year and a half after the *New York Times*/CBS News poll discussed in table 4.1 and several days after the October 16 march, a 1995 poll by *Time*/CNN News illustrated how the context in which a survey is taken may shape opinion.

Table 4.2 displays favorability evaluations of Farrakhan and four other prominent black leaders, Jesse Jackson, Colin Powell, Clarence Thomas, and former NAACP President Benjamin Chavis. Compared to the 1994 survey, two things stand out: (1) among blacks, the number of those declining to express an opinion dropped sharply, from 30% to 18% (not shown in the table); (2) among whites, it increased from 18% to 31%. How is this dynamic to be accounted for? First, it may show the impact of a slight change in question wording; the 1994 poll in-

Table 4.2   Attitudes toward Minister Farrakhan, Compared to Four Other Prominent African American Leaders, October 1995 (% with Favorable Opinion)

	Blacks	Whites	Gap	Gulf	Chasm
Louis Farrakhan	52%	6%			46
Jesse Jackson	90	58		32	
Colin Powell	63	79	16		
Benjamin Chavis	32	6		26	
Clarence Thomas	31	36	—		

Source: *Time*/CNN, October 1995.

cluded an "undecided" choice in addition to the "not familiar with" or "haven't heard enough about" to have an opinion. Almost certainly, a couple of days after the widely publicized march, Farrakhan had become better known but not—at least among whites—better liked. Rather, the effect of the march among whites was to increase those undecided.

As in the 1994 poll, in the 1995 poll the chasm in black-white unfavorability remained unchanged—46 after the march, 44 before. The percentage of whites with a favorable opinion of the minister remained trivial. However, the march apparently resulted in a substantial increase in favorability among blacks—from 36% in early 1994 to 52% by October 1995.

Again in the 1995 poll (but not shown in the table) is the tendency observed in the 1994 poll for middle-class, college-educated blacks to be more favorable toward Farrakhan. But unlike in 1994 when there were no age effects, the young (18–29) are now more favorable, especially when compared with people 60 and older (a gulf of 34 between the young and the old). Since he began the revitalization of the Nation in the 1980s, Farrakhan has targeted young people (see note 3). At least in the context of the march's aftermath, it appears he has had some success.

A number of observers—including prominent black women—criticized the male exclusiveness of the call for a million man march, although several prominent black women endorsed and spoke at the march.[4] Apparently, however, the all-male march did not engender strong gender effects. Farrakhan's favorability ratings went up dramatically among both men and women, although there is a modest tendency for men to be more favorable.

Jesse Jackson is the preeminent African American leader of the post–civil rights era (Frady, 1996; Smith, 1996: chaps. 9–11; Walters and Smith, 1999: 197–221), a consensus leader among blacks with a near 90% favorable rating. In the context of this poll, he is also viewed favorably by most whites, but note here there is a gulf of 32 in black-white favorability toward Jackson. General Powell approaches the status of a racially transcendent leader, being somewhat more popular among whites (79% favorable) than blacks (63%).

Louis Farrakhan is the most influential black nationalist leader. Clarence Thomas is the most powerful African American conservative. And Benjamin Chavis, at the time of the survey, was the Million Man March coordinator; but he had previously headed the NAACP (National Association for the Advancement of Colored People), the most important civil rights organization.[5]

In the context of the march, blacks were much more predisposed toward the black nationalist leader than they were toward the black conservative Supreme Court jurist or the former head of the liberal integrationist NAACP (although half of blacks did not know enough about Chavis to express an opinion). Thomas, who at the time of this survey had been on the Supreme Court for four years, is generally viewed unfavorably by both blacks and whites. There is also a modest white gender gap of 14 (not shown in table), perhaps due to the Anita Hill sexual harassment allegations or to his hard-line stance on reversing the *Roe v. Wade* (1973) abortion decision.

Sharpening our insights into opinion on Farrakhan's leadership, we present in table 4.3 data on perspectives on his leadership qualities and then in table 4.4 opinions on the march. The data in table 4.3 show that Farrakhan is a divisive leader, dividing blacks and whites but also dividing blacks. A majority of whites viewed him as a racist bigot, but so did more than a third of blacks. Only a handful of whites said they admired Farrakhan, whereas 39% of blacks did. Similarly, hardly any whites said they agreed with his views, but also only about one-third of blacks said they did. Two-thirds of blacks and nearly half of whites thought his views were separatist rather than "moderate."

Table 4.3   Attitudes toward Minister Farrakhan by Race, October 1995 (% Agreeing)

	Blacks	Whites	Gap	Gulf	Chasm
Think Farrakhan is separatist*	63%	45%	18		
Generally agree with his position	36	5		31	
Positive force in black community	51	16		35	
Personally admire	39	4		35	
Good for black community	62	20			42
A bigot/racist	37	54	17		
Speaks truth	58	12			46
Effective leader	63	35		28	
Role model for youth	56	12			44

Source: *Time*/CNN, October 1995.

*The question read: Do you think Farrakhan is more of a racial moderate or a racial separatist who believes in keeping blacks and whites separate?

Nevertheless 35% of whites said he was an effective leader, as did almost two-thirds of blacks. Also, in spite of their reservations, more than half of blacks thought that he was good for the black community and a role model for young people. In sum, although there were gulfs and chasms between blacks and whites in opinion on Farrakhan, there were also differences among blacks.[6]

Finally, there were clear although modest class differences (measured by education) and somewhat stronger age effects but no gender differences among blacks in opinions on Farrakhan. College-educated blacks and young people tended to be more admiring of Farrakhan than those with less education or the elderly. For example, 71% of college-educated blacks agreed that Farrakhan was an effective leader (compared to 61% of high school graduates); and a striking 70% of 18–30-year-olds compared to only 33% of those 60 and older agreed with this evaluation.

The stated goals of the Million Man March were for black men to "atone" for their misdeeds as husbands and fathers and to take personal responsibility for their families and communities (Madhubuti and Karenga, 1996: 140–69). As the figures in table 4.4 show, 84% of blacks but also 62% of whites indicated agreement with these broadly stated objectives (we assume here that they were aware of these stated goals because the question did not state them but asked simply whether respondents agreed or disagreed with the objectives). Indeed, table 4.4 shows much more agreement across the color line about the march than about the man who called it. The areas of gulf-chasm differences concern the official estimates of the march's size and whether the march would increase Farrakhan's influence. Blacks and whites agreed that the march would increase Farrakhan's influence; 48% of blacks said they would like to see this happen, but only 9% of whites said they would.[7] The National Park Service estimated the size of the march at 400,000, whereas march organizers and several independent sources (see *Jet*, 1995) put the size at a million or more. This difference elicited a race chasm of 44—62% of blacks but only 18% of whites agreed that the government underestimated the march's size.[8]

Table 4.4   Opinions on the Million Man March by Race (% Agreeing)

	Blacks	Whites	Gap	Gulf	Chasm
Goals of march	84%	62%	22		
March will increase race tensions	34	35	—		
Government understated size of march	62	18			44
Farrakhan more influential in black community	57	49	—		
Would like to see Farrakhan more influential	48	9		39	

Source: *Time*/CNN, October 1995.

THE SUPREME COURT NOMINATION AND
CONFIRMATION OF CLARENCE THOMAS

From a controversial, racially divisive leader and context, we turn now to one less racially divisive—Supreme Court Justice Clarence Thomas. On July 1, 1991, President Bush nominated Clarence Thomas to the Supreme Court as the successor to Thurgood Marshall, the legendary civil rights lawyer and the Court's first and only black member. Thomas, then forty-three, was black but conservative, having embraced the entire right-wing agenda on race as well as other domestic matters (see Phelps and Winternitz, 1992). Feminist leaders suspected that Thomas was an opponent of abortion rights as promulgated in *Roe v. Wade*. A former chair of the Equal Employment Opportunity Commission (EEOC) at the time of his nomination, Thomas was a judge on the District of Columbia Court of Appeals. With the Thomas nomination, Bush—perhaps deliberately—created a dilemma, a conundrum for black leaders and their liberal allies, who had insisted that it was important for Bush to select a black to replace Marshall. But they strongly opposed Thomas on ideological grounds. However, if Thomas was defeated, Bush aides implied he would nominate an equally conservative white, leaving the Court without any black presence.

In the end most black leaders opposed the Thomas nomination. However, his approval seemed certain until Anita Hill, then a little-known law professor at the University of Oklahoma, alleged Thomas sexually harassed her while she was employed at the Department of Education (where Thomas briefly served as an assistant secretary) and the EEOC. These allegations were made several days before the Senate was scheduled to vote on confirmation. Under intense pressure from liberals, blacks, and especially feminist leaders, the Senate agreed to hold hearings on Hill's charges prior to voting. For two days over a weekend, the country watched on national television as Hill, Thomas, and others traded charges and countercharges about sex, sexism, race, and racism, including titillating tales about pubic hairs and "long dong silver."[9]

We utilize four polls by the *New York Times*/CBS News to analyze race opinion on the Thomas nomination and the Hill allegations. The first was conducted during the first week of September 1991, after the Senate Judiciary Committee completed its hearings on the nomination but prior to Hill's allegations. The next three polls were conducted after her allegations were made public. They were part of a panel study; that is, the same people were interviewed on three different dates—October 8, 13, and 14. This panel technique is useful in this short time frame (the short period avoids the problem of attrition that often mars panel studies conducted over extended periods of time) to study the dynamics of opinion formation and change—specifically, how the public reacted to Hill's initial charges and the two days of televised hearings.[10]

The hearings reached a huge audience. Conducted on a Saturday and Sunday, 88% of whites and 96% of blacks reported watching the live broadcast of the hearings. But prior to the Hill-Thomas sex hearings, the American people apparently had paid relatively little attention to the Judiciary Committee's hearings on confirmation. At least that is the inference to be drawn from the data displayed in table 4.5, which shows about 60% of both blacks and whites saying they did not know enough about Thomas to rate him in terms of favorability or to say whether he should be confirmed. The hearings had been thoroughly covered in the national media (although they were not televised on the commercial networks), but apparently the controversy surrounding the nomination had little salience for much of the public.

In general, throughout the controversy, there was remarkable consensus in opinion across the color line. The only area on which there was a gulf in opinion was on whether it was important to have a black on the Court—80% of blacks said it was very important, but only 48% of whites. A major source of black-leadership opposition to Thomas was his opposition to affirmative action—many blacks argued that because Thomas was one who had benefited from affirmative action, his position was a betrayal of the race (see Walters, 1999). As table 4.5 shows, both blacks and whites agreed that Thomas's nomination was a result of affirmative action; that is, 50% of blacks and 43% of whites agreed that the "main reason" Bush nominated Thomas was because of his race rather than because he was "the best-qualified person." But Thomas's opposition to affirmative action was not especially bothersome. Only 8% of whites agreed that Thomas's opposition to affirmative action meant he was "turning his back on his own people" but also only 26% of blacks, a modest gap of 18.

Although most Americans did not know enough to have an opinion on the confirmation, of those who did, most favored confirmation—blacks by a margin of 25% to 16%, whites by 29% to 12%. Both races agreed that the Court that Thomas was about to join was too conservative; however, majorities of blacks and whites indicated they did not think Thomas's confirmation would make much change in the ideological direction of the Court.

What is most striking about this initial poll of opinion on Thomas is the admitted ignorance of the public about the Court and Thomas, this in spite of the fact that news about Thomas and the Court was pervasive throughout the summer. Why did the public ignore this controversy, which so deeply divided the elite? Perhaps because only a tiny handful of respondents thought Thomas's appointment would have a major effect on what the Court would do.[11]

Context, as we have said throughout this book, matters for understanding the public's opinions; and we know that nothing gets the public's attention like sex. Thus, Anita Hill's allegations dramatically altered public awareness of the nomination. As we said earlier, nearly 90% of both blacks and whites watched the

Table 4.5   Racial Differences in Opinion on the Supreme Court Nomination of Clarence Thomas at the Conclusion of Senate Confirmation Hearings, September 3–5, 1991

	Blacks	Whites	Gap	Gulf
Favorable Opinion	20%	28%	—	
Unfavorable Opinion	19	10		
Don't Know	62	61		
Should Senate confirm?				
Yes	25	29	—	
No	16	12		
Don't Know	59	60		
If Thomas confirmed, court will become more:				
Liberal	8	9	—	
Conservative	32	37		
No Change	61	60		
Thomas nominated mainly because of his race (yes)	50	43	—	
Important to have black on court	80	48		32
Thomas's opposition to affirmative action means turning back on his own people	26	8	18	
Supreme Court is too:				
Liberal	28	37	—	
Conservative	63	50		
About Right	9	13		
Impact of Thomas on Court, if confirmed:				
Great	22	11	11	
Some	29	46		
Not Much	48	43		

Source: *New York Times*/CBS News, September 3–5, 1991.

televised weekend hearings. Unlike many other of the controversies we examine in this book, this one in general elicited interracial consensus. The consensus was maintained after the Hill allegations.

In table 4.6, we see that pluralities of blacks and whites favored confirmation, although relatively high percentages remained undecided. And only 19% of blacks and 23% of whites opposed confirmation. This is probably because most people did not believe Hill. Bare majorities (48% of blacks, 53% of whites) did think her charges should be taken seriously, and substantial majorities agreed that if the charges were true Thomas should not be confirmed. The problem was that most Americans did not believe Hill; only 34% of blacks and 35% of whites agreed

Table 4.6 Racial Differences in Opinion on Anita Hill and Clarence Thomas after Initial Hill Allegations, October 8, 1991

	Blacks	*Whites*	*Gap*
Should Senate confirm? (% yes)	42%	44%	—
Are Hill's allegations probably true? (% yes)	34	35	—
Should Hill's allegations be taken seriously? (% yes)	48	53	—
If charges are true should Senate confirm (% yes)	35	22	13

Source: *New York Times*/CBS News, October 8, 1991.

that Hill's allegations were "probably true." Strikingly, there were no statistically significant differences between men and women, between the young and the old, and between the college educated and those with only a high school education. Although white women were somewhat more likely to oppose confirmation, black women were somewhat more likely to support it; but these differences were modest.

The completion of the hearings did not alter this consensus. As table 4.7 shows,

Table 4.7 Racial Differences in Opinion on Clarence Thomas and Anita Hill at Completion of Senate Hearings on Sexual Harassment, October 13, 1991

	Blacks	*Whites*	*Gap*
Opinion of Hill			
Favorable	16%	20%	—
Unfavorable	63	68	—
No opinion	22	13	—
Was Thomas telling the truth?			
Yes	37%	35%	—
No	54	54	—
No opinion	12	9	—
Was Hill telling the truth?			
Yes	11	17	—
No	56	48	—
No opinion	33	35	—
Did Senate Committee treat Hill fairly? (% yes)	88	90	
Did Senate Committee treat Thomas fairly? (% yes)	63	75	12
Who do you believe more? (% saying Thomas)	71	67	
If charges are true, should Senate confirm? (% yes)	35	22	13
When Senate votes tomorrow, if there is doubt about truth, should Thomas be confirmed? (% yes)*	70	58	12

Source: *New York Times*/CBS News, October 13, 1991.

*This item is from the final, October 14, poll.

respondents, both black and white, believed Thomas rather than Hill and had a more favorable impression of him than her. Thus, in the final poll in the three-panel wave conducted on October 14, the day before the Senate vote, 70% of blacks and 58% of whites favored confirmation. There were again some modest race-gender effects—64% of white men and 69% of black men favored confirmation; 71% of black women but a bare 50% of white women favored confirmation. On October 15, the Senate, by a 52-to-48 vote, confirmed Thomas as the second African American on the nation's highest Court.

The controversy over the Thomas nomination recalls a similar battle when President Reagan nominated the conservative jurist Robert Bork to the Supreme Court (see Bronner, 1983). Bork was eventually defeated, largely because southern, conservative Democrats voted against him. These conservative senators voted against Bork in part because of the opposition of women and especially of blacks—not just black and feminist leaders but also black and female mass opinion. A similar outcome probably would have been the case in the Thomas vote (Phelps and Winternitz, 1992: 392–415). But, unlike the Bork case, black mass opinion did not follow the black elite, and the opinion of white women was about equally divided. Thus, southern conservative Democrats may have concluded that opposition to Thomas's nomination was unwarranted, given his strong support among blacks, especially black women.

To the extent that Hill's last-minute allegations were a desperate strategic ploy by Thomas's opponents to block his nomination—as to some extent it surely was—it backfired. If the allegations had been believed by women and black women in particular, then the strategy might have worked. But given that Hill was not believed, the major effect of her allegations was to increase public knowledge of Thomas and to increase support for his confirmation.[12]

Finally, blacks supported Thomas in spite of his conservatism and his opposition to affirmative action because, apparently, they judged it was important to have a black—any black—on the Court and because they did not think his appointment would make much difference in shaping the Court's direction. We will say more about this conundrum for contemporary black leadership later in this chapter.[13]

GENERAL COLIN POWELL: A TRANSRACIAL LEADER

One of the interesting by-products of the Persian Gulf War was the emergence of General Colin Powell as a national leader and prospective presidential candidate (Williams, 1994). Powell, as chairman of the Joint Chiefs of Staff, was one of the handful of key decision makers during the Gulf crisis and a principal defender of the Bush policy on national television (see Woodward, 1991). This was a historic development.—the first time a black person had played a major role in decision making on war and peace.

For much of its history, the American foreign policy establishment was almost the exclusive preserve of white men (until the end of World War II, white Protestant males of upper-status Ivy League background).[14] Since the 1960s, a few blacks have served in the executive foreign-policy-making apparatus: Carl Rowan, Director of the United States Information Agency under President Johnson, was the first black to participate in meetings of the high-level National Security Council). And Andrew Young and Donald McHenry served as UN ambassadors during the Carter administration. The roles of these men, however, were marginal to overall, national-security decision making. Powell, however, was a key decision maker in the Reagan administration, where he served for two years as National Security Adviser; and in the Bush administration, he was a pivotal participant in Persian Gulf decision making (Woodward, 1991).

When Bush was elected president, he reportedly offered Powell a choice of two other top foreign policy jobs: director of the Central Intelligence Agency (CIA) and deputy secretary of state. Powell declined both, opting instead to return to his military career. A year later Bush appointed him chairman of the Joint Chiefs, the youngest person and the first black to hold the top military job. Powell became well known to the public during the Gulf crisis. Although he reportedly opposed immediately going to war, favoring the Democratic congressional leadership position of a strategy of economic sanction (Woodward, 1991), once the decision for war was made, Powell managed the development and the implementation of the strategy that resulted in the rapid defeat of the Iraqi military. His poised and self-confident defense of the war on television and the quick victory of the American forces made Powell something of a national hero.

After two terms at the Joint Chiefs, Powell retired from the Army, wrote his memoirs (Powell, 1995), engaged in a widely publicized national book tour, announced he was a Republican, and briefly considered running for president in 1996. Although he eventually decided not to run, for a time he was among the leading prospective candidates,[15] popular with the national press and among leaders of both political parties.[16]

Although Powell was popular among white politicians and media elites, among the black political establishment his rise to national prominence was met with skepticism or ambivalence (see Gates, 1995). This reaction to Powell among elements of the black establishment may be traced to his roles in the Gulf War, the Vietnam War, and the invasions of Panama and Grenada; his close association with Reagan and Bush; and his affiliation with the Republican Party. One prominent black scholar even described Powell as "un-Negro" because of his alleged "white middle-class demeanor" (Walters, 1995).

In September 1995, at the height of the speculation about a Powell run for the presidency, Gallup conducted a poll for *USA Today*/CNN News assessing Powell's prospects as a candidate and his perceived leadership qualities. In table 4.8, the data are displayed on three hypothetical matchups in the 1996 election. In the first matchup between President Clinton and Republican Senator Robert Dole, the familiar partisan chasm of 40 plus is evident—93% of blacks preferred Clinton, compared to 49% of whites. However, when the Republican nominee is Powell, the partisan chasm shrinks to a modest gap of 14. A majority of blacks (54%) still prefer the Democrat Clinton but support for the Republican Party with Powell as its candidate increases nearly sixfold among blacks. Among whites the addition of Powell to the Republican ticket has only a modest impact, with support for Clinton declining from 49% to 40%.

In a three-way race between Republican Dole, Democrat Clinton, and Powell as an Independent, the black vote is evenly divided between Clinton and Powell, whereas among whites there is a virtual three-way tie (blacks by a margin of 71% to 42% were more likely to favor Powell running as an Independent rather than as a Republican).

Men, black and white, were more likely than women to favor Powell (60% of black women, for example, said they would have voted for Clinton in a race against Powell, compared to 47% of black men). There was also a slight tendency for college-educated respondents of both races to favor Powell. But the most striking difference is with respect to age among blacks. Blacks forty-five and older gave

Table 4.8   Racial Differences in Support for Colin Powell as a Presidential Candidate in the 1996 Elections

	Blacks	Whites	Gap	Gulf	Chasm
If the election was between Democrat Bill Clinton and Republican Bob Dole:					
Vote for Clinton	93%	49%			44
If the election was between Democrat Bill Clinton and Colin Powell as the Republican candidate:					
Vote for Clinton	54	40	14		
If the election was between Democrat Bill Clinton, Republican Bob Dole, and Independent Colin Powell:					
Vote for Clinton	45	32			
Vote for Dole	9	36			
Vote for Powell	47	32	15		

Source: *Gallup*/*USA Today*/CNN, September 1995.

Powell only 27% of their vote in a race against Clinton, whereas younger blacks (eighteen to forty-four) gave him 42%.[17]

The results of this poll *suggest* that putting Powell on the Republican ticket *may* have substantially altered the partisan race chasm and that in a three-way race Powell (with substantial black support) *might* have deprived Clinton of the presidency or even won the office himself. We emphasize *may, suggest,* and *might.* These poll data from the fall of 1995—more than a year before the election—should obviously be viewed with extreme skepticism. The dynamics of a hard-fought presidential campaign would almost surely have altered these results, although in what directions and to whose benefit we cannot know. Powell at this time had been almost free of any kind of criticism. Indeed, his press coverage then was almost wholly laudatory. Powell had not staked out positions on important issues—except for support for affirmative action and abortion rights—and thus poll respondents were reacting to a symbol as much as to a possible president.

In table 4.9, data are displayed that compare opinions of blacks and whites on Powell's leadership capabilities and his capacity to handle the country's problems. Blacks and whites have similar assessments of Powell's ability to handle foreign policy, to provide leadership, and to represent moral values. It is interesting that, even on his capacity to handle race relations, there is no racial difference, in spite of the media commentary and reporting that constantly suggested that Powell's race would make him more effective in bridging the country's racial divide. To the contrary, both blacks and whites thought that Powell's race would make it harder for him to lead the country—80% of whites, 64% of blacks. On other issues—improving the economy and handling medicare—black respondents were more positive than whites. On these issues, however, the key finding was that most

Table 4.9   Racial Differences in Confidence about Colin Powell's Ability to Handle the Country's Problems

	Great Deal of Confidence			
	Blacks	*Whites*	*Gap*	*Gulf*
Race relations	47	46	—	
Foreign policy	56	52	—	
The economy	38	15		23
Deficit reduction	12	24	12	
Medicare	38	16		22
Provide leadership	60	58	—	
Represent moral values	45	45	—	

Source: *Gallup*/CNN, September 1995.

respondents (65% of whites, 75% of blacks) indicated they were unsure whether Powell's views agreed with their own—a sensible position because on most issues Powell had not stated positions.

Until its end, the Persian Gulf War divided the country by color. The quick and decisive victory of the American forces bridged, at least temporarily, the racial gulfs and chasms and in the process produced perhaps for the first time in the nation's history a genuine national leader who was black—a political leader capable of bridging the race chasm in partisanship and in presidential choice. Although there were some gaps between the races, for a moment, General Powell transcended race.

CONCLUSION: THE CONUNDRUM OF POST–CIVIL RIGHTS ERA BLACK LEADERSHIP

In *African American Leadership*, Walters and Smith (1999) argued that post–civil rights era black leadership is in a conundrum. First, there is the constant dynamic tension in a racially stratified society between the "black perspective" on an event and the attempt by whites to impose the dominant perspective. This dynamic tension is as old as the black freedom struggle itself. However, in the post–civil rights era, this tension has a new dimension for black leadership. Prior to the civil rights revolution of the 1960s, black leadership was confined to leading the black community—to mobilizing its resources for purposes of internal community development and in pursuit of its interests in the larger society. Today, black leadership is bifurcated; that is, although some blacks may continue to lead blacks as the primary focus of their work, others seek to lead America in general, as governors, mayors, justices of the Supreme Court, or head of the Joint Chiefs of Staff. Both of these leadership types separately and together create the conundrum that is evident in the three cases examined in this chapter.

Black leaders—those people who see the primary focus of their work as mobilizing the resources of the black community and articulating its interests—to be effective are likely to arouse antagonisms in the larger community, and such leaders are also likely to find it difficult to move from leading blacks to leading America. This may be seen in the case of Jesse Jackson, a mainstream black leader but one who is viewed by many whites as an extreme left-liberal, which, of course, he is in the context of the broader currents of American politics. This view, Jackson's race and racism notwithstanding, is sufficient to explain the difficulties he faces in trying to transcend his race leadership role to become a leader of America.

If Jackson is evidence of this conundrum, the leadership of Louis Farrakhan epitomizes it. Jesse Jackson is a mainstream consensus black leader. Louis Farrakhan represents one of its extremes—militant black nationalism. The more effectively he articulates the rage of the black community, the more he alienates whites and mainstream black America. Myrdal recognized this conundrum—what he called dilemma—more than fifty years ago when he noted that the most effective way to organize the black masses was in "a strongly emotional race—chauvinistic protest appeal." But, he wrote, "This is a real dilemma. For white support will be denied to emotional Negro chauvinism when it takes organizational and political form" (Myrdal, [1944], 1962: 749). Thus, it is probably true that no other contemporary black leader—not Jesse Jackson or all the black members of Congress and black mayors together—except Farrakhan could have brought a million black men to Washington. Yet Farrakhan's leadership creates chasms between the races as well as amongst blacks. Hardly any whites view him favorably and only half of blacks do. This is a real dilemma, a real conundrum.

Turning from black leaders to those blacks who lead America, one observes another dilemma. Blacks certainly want to see blacks in leadership positions throughout America. Indeed, this was a major goal of the civil rights movement—integration of blacks into all walks of American life. Yet to effectively lead America requires transcending race, transcending the black perspective and its interests to embrace the range of races and perspectives that constitute America. Yet when a black leader of America does this, he is frequently accused by other blacks of "estrangement from his blackness" or betrayal of the race. This, too, is a real conundrum, observed in some of the commentary when Douglas Wilder was elected governor of Virginia (Smith, 1990a; Walters, 1992), in the negative reaction of black leaders to the nomination of the conservative Clarence Thomas to the Supreme Court by a conservative president, or in their ambivalent, skeptical response to the moderate Colin Powell as a possible U.S. president. Both of these black leaders of America (Thomas and Powell) were more popular among whites than blacks, although mass opinion was not nearly as hostile as elite opinion—yet another conundrum.

Finally, Walters and Smith in *African American Leadership* predicted that gender relations were likely to become an increasingly important and perhaps divisive issue in black leadership and society. Two of the controversies examined in this chapter shed some light on gender relations and leadership: (1) Farrakhan and his Million Man March and (2) the Hill–Thomas controversy. Because of Farrakhan's overt, religion-rooted adherence to patriarchy in the governance of the Nation, his support for the traditional family, his opposition to abortion, and his call for a men- only march, many black feminists and others were critical of Farrakhan and his march. However, with respect to Farrakhan and the march, no gender gap is observed. Black women were no more likely to express hostility toward Farrakhan or the march than men were. Rather, differences about Farrakhan are based more on education and age than gender.

In the Hill–Thomas controversy, a black woman charged a black man with sexual harassment; but black women were no more likely to believe Professor

Chapter Four

Hill than black men were. Indeed, to the extent that there was a gender gap, black women were more skeptical about Hill's charges than black men were, and the women were more supportive of Thomas's confirmation after the hearings than black men were. Finally, with respect to gender, we should recall that black women were much more skeptical than black men about General Powell, owing perhaps to their strong opposition to America's wars generally and the Persian Gulf War specifically.

NOTES

1. In the past several years there have been several book-length studies of Minister Farrakhan and the Nation. See Magida (1996); Singh (1997); and Gardeau (1996). The most comprehensive and balanced of these studies is Gardell's (see also Mamiya, 1982 and Smith, 1996: 100–105).

2. Black nationalism is an ideology with many permutations or varieties; but at its core it involves a skepticism about whites and about the possibilities of integration and equality; and its adherents tend to favor self-reliance, group solidarity, and some forms of racial autonomy, although not necessarily territorial separatism (Stuckey, 1987; Smith, 1992).

3. The social basis of the organization is the urban, lower middle class and, in increasing numbers, alienated young people attracted to nationalism by the heroic image of Malcolm X and the music of several rap groups that employ themes from Malcolm's and Farrakhan's speeches in their lyrics.

4. For a documentary record of the march, including the speeches, position papers, and commentaries, see Madhubuti and Karenga (1996); and for data on the opinions of the men who attended the march, see McCormick (1997).

5. Chavis had been ousted as head of the NAACP because of allegations of sexual and financial improprieties, although his nationalist inclinations also probably played a role (see Lusanne and Steele, 1994, and Smith, 1996: 90–94). He was subsequently appointed by Farrakhan as National Coordinator of the march. Later, he converted to Islam and became a minister in the Nation.

6. Apparently the march did not markedly alter opinion among blacks. For example, a *Time* poll in January 1994 found that essentially the same percentage of blacks who rated Farrakhan as an effective leader (65%) also rated him as one who speaks the truth (63%) and one who is good for the black community (62%). Also, as in the postmarch survey, a similar percentage viewed him as a racist bigot (see Henry, 1994).

7. In the views of the editors of *Time*, the nation's most widely read news weekly, the march did increase Farrakhan's influence. After the march, *Time* editors named Farrakhan one of the nation's twenty-five most influential Americans, writing, "Those who arrived at the national mall had come to move beyond the pieties of 'we shall overcome' and to bear witness to their experience of tragic social and economic dislocations that have touched the poor, the well-to-do, and the brightest and best among them. And they came to do so at the fiery beckoning of Louis Farrakhan" (*Time*, 1996: 67).

8. Blacks and whites agreed also on the relative historical significance of the march. When asked which march was more significant, the Million Man or the 1963 March led by Dr. King, only 6% of whites and 18% of blacks said the Million Man March.

9. Professor Hill claimed that Justice Thomas had placed pubic hairs on a can of coke in his office and referred to his penis as "long dong silver." "Long Dong Silver" is the title of a popular blues song by Denice LaSalle.

10. Because the October 14 poll results do not differ from those of October 13, we only analyze one question from the October 14 poll, one dealing with opinion on the final confirmation vote.

11. We should note that in general most Americans know little about the Supreme Court or its justices. A *Washington Post* poll, for example, found that although 59% of Americans could name the Three Stooges, only 17% could name three of the nine justices (only 8% could name the Chief Justice). See Biskupic, 1995.

12. We refer here to the short-term effect of the allegations on Thomas's confirmation. The major long-term effect of the Hill–Thomas controversy was to increase public awareness and sensitivity to workplace sexual harassment. The controversy generated a modest literature. See, for example, Brock, 1993; Morrison, 1992; Flax, 1998; and Hill's (1997) memoir. The Morrison-edited volume attempted to place the controversy in a larger historical, psychological, and cultural analysis of racial and sexual politics in the United States.

Also, we should note that some observers have stated that after the hearings and Thomas's confirmation, opinion shifted toward believing Professor Hill rather than Justice Thomas. We were not able to locate any poll or survey data supporting this alleged opinion shift. However, the most detailed study of the Hill–Thomas controversy concluded that Professor Hill was probably telling the truth in the charges she made during the Senate hearings (see Mayer and Abramson, 1994).

13. In his several years on the Court, Justice Thomas has arguably become the most conservative of the justices.

14. As late as 1998, African Americans accounted for only 2.7% of U.S. diplomats. For a history of black integration of the foreign service after World War II, see Krenn (1998).

15. Polls taken from the fall of 1995 through early 1996 asking who would make the best president showed Powell consistently in the lead. These early polls also showed Powell winning the early New Hampshire primary.

16. Powell's positions in support of abortion rights and affirmative action made him not so popular among right-wing Republicans,whose criticisms during this period of speculation about his candidacy were, in general, muted.

17. This finding is consistent with several recent studies that show that younger blacks are more alienated from the Democratic party and inclined toward an independent or Republican stance in voting behavior. See, for example, Tate (1994).

5

Rumors and Conspiracies: Justified Paranoia?

In studying race differences in attitudes and opinions, a fertile though often ne-
glected area for inquiry is conspiracies and rumors of conspiracies and their preva-
lence in the African American community. It is extensively documented that African Americans tend to explain aspects of their subordinate place in the United
States on the basis of conspiracies by whites. Again, this notion has been thoroughly explored in books and articles; browsing any large, urban, black-oriented
bookstore, one will encounter more than a hundred titles devoted to the subject.
Yet in these many works on conspiracies and African Americans, there is very
little systematic data on the extent to which blacks, compared to whites, embrace
conspiracies and rumors of conspiracies. Rather, most of these studies are histories, studies in folklore, literary analyses, or the work of journalists or popular
writers. In this chapter, therefore, we can break some new ground in this area of
research by first bringing to bear a number of polls and surveys on conspiracies.

Patricia Turner's *I Heard It through the Grapevine* (1993) is probably the best
book-length treatment of this subject. Although in it she dealt with some admit-
tedly preposterous rumors involving conspiracies against blacks (for example, that
the Ku Klux Klan owned Church's Fried Chicken and the company that manufac-
tured the popular soft drink Tropical Fantasy, and that these products contained
secret ingredients that sterilized black males), she also dealt with more plausible
ones—possible conspiracies to assassinate important national leaders (Martin
Luther King Jr., Malcolm X, and John F. Kennedy) or Central Intelligence Agency
(CIA) plans to channel drugs into the black community. In her work, Turner wrote:

I defend the somewhat controversial position that they [rumors of conspiracies] do not necessarily reflect pathological preoccupations among African Americans. Rather, I make the case that these rumors and contemporary legends often function as tools of resistance for many of the folk who share of them. (1993: 4)

Turner's central thesis was that rumors and conspiracy theories in the African American community are rooted in slavery and racial subordination. She argued that the rumors served a defensive function for the African American community, a cultural weapon in the struggle against racism. She concluded her work by writing:

Attention to the content of the rumors, however unsettling, merely detracts attention from the function these rumors serve for those who believe them. The rumors themselves do not cause the wounds from which African Americans suffer—racism, inequality, and prejudice do. Like a scab that forms over a sore, the rumors are unattractive but vital mechanisms by which the cultural body attempts to protect itself from subsequent infection (1993: 225)

—justified paranoia, in other words.

In a less sympathetic work, Pipes wrote, "Conspiracy theories may well be the most prevalent in black America" (1997: 2). Although Pipes argued that "conspiracism" is potentially dangerous in a democratic society, he contended that it is based in a sense of alienation and disaffection. Pipes wrote that a survey of conspiracy theories in America showed that they tend to come disproportionately from two groups—the "politically disaffected" and the "culturally suspicious." And:

Among the politically disaffected the black community and the hard right are most overtly conspiracy-theory minded. Both dislike the existing order and offer radical ideas about changing it; both resort to an outlook that depends heavily on the existence of powerful forces engaged in plots. (1997: 2)

The tendency toward conspiracism in the black community may plausibly be viewed as a cultural defense mechanism and a product of alienation from the established political order; it may also reflect recent historical experiences and memories, such as the FBI plots against Dr. Martin Luther King Jr. (Garrow, 1981) and the infamous Tuskegee experiments involving withholding treatment from black men infected with syphilis (Jones, 1982). This phenomenon may also be a product of the relative absence of trust of others, a distinctive attribute of contemporary African American culture that we discussed earlier. As we indicated in chapter 1, this contemporary cultural attribute has deep historical roots going back to the slave culture.

Jewelle Taylor Gibbs, a clinical psychologist and professor of social policy at the University of California, Berkeley, wrote (1996: 237) that there are four major categories of conspiracies in the African American community.[1] They include:

1. *Criminalization and drugs*—theories that drugs are deliberately placed in the black community in order to criminalize it and destroy its capacity for resistance.

2. *Contamination and disease*—theories that portray blacks as guinea pigs or victims in the tests of new viruses and the spread of disease.

3. *Destruction of black leaders and organizations*—theories that the government deliberately targets black leaders and prominent black persons (especially men) for defamation and destruction.

4. *Racial and cultural genocide*—theories that the government and other white groups are involved in various strategies such as forced sterilization and involuntary birth control as means of eradicating black people.

Gibbs noted that these conspiracy "motifs and myths" are "widely disseminated in the black community through the black media, music, political leaders, churches, and civic and social organizations" (1996: 236–37).

It is with this background and these frames of reference that we analyze available survey data on conspiracy opinions in the United States. We analyze three types of conspiracism: (1) a set of conspiracy theories that are directly related to African Americans, such as the notion that the United States government deliberately makes drugs available in the black community; that AIDS is part of a conspiracy to destroy blacks; and that the government deliberately targets prominent blacks for defamation and destruction; (2) theories unrelated to blacks, such as whether the government was involved in the assassination of President Kennedy; (3) beliefs in the paranormal, such as whether angels, devils, or UFOs exist. The second and third types of questions allow us to place opinions on conspiracies related to blacks in a broader context. Are blacks merely more likely than whites to believe in conspiracies against blacks, or is there a more general tendency among blacks toward conspiracism? Similarly, are blacks more likely to believe in the rationally or scientifically undemonstrable, such as the paranormal?

CONSPIRACIES AGAINST BLACKS

Drugs

Perhaps the most abiding rumor of conspiracy in the African American community, particularly since the late 1960s, has been the idea that the United States government—most frequently and specifically the CIA—has been responsible for the widespread availability of drugs in black neighborhoods. This idea has been advanced for years by black activists, especially the Nation of Islam in its widely circulated weekly newspaper, the *Final Call*. This drug conspiracy theme has also been advanced in black popular music and in books, articles, and pamphlets. For example, the movie *Black Panther* has as its final scene a plot by government agents to flood black neighborhoods with heroin and other drugs as a means of preventing the reemergence of the Panthers or other radical, revolutionary organizations.

These rumors became more widespread in the 1980s when a new drug called crack cocaine became widely available in black communities across the country.[2] This inexpensive (compared to powdered cocaine), highly addictive derivative of powdered cocaine resulted in an explosion of crack addicts, drug-related gangs, and violence. This was followed by the passage of draconian drug laws and the jailing of large numbers of black men and more and more black women (see the discussion in chapter 6 on blacks and the criminal justice system), leading many blacks to describe the war on drugs as a war on blacks (Harris, 1990).

These rumors were seemingly confirmed when in August 1996 the *San Jose Mercury News* published a three-part series of investigative reports by correspondent Gary Webb that strongly suggested that the CIA was indeed responsible for the manufacture and distribution of crack by Los Angeles street gangs, as a means for the agency to finance the Contras' covert war against the leftist Sandinista government of Nicaragua (see Webb, 1996). The establishment press, including the *Washington Post*, the *New York Times*, and the *Los Angeles Times*, attempted to discredit Webb's story, finding, as the *New York Times* put it, "scant proof" to support the CIA-crack connection (Suro and Pincus, 1996; Katz, 1996; Golden, 1996).

After denials by CIA director John Deutch and after extensive criticism from other newspapers as well as members of Congress, the *San Jose Mercury News* conducted what it called an internal reexamination of Webb's story and concluded that parts of it were an "oversimplification" and that there was not "proof" that "top CIA officials" knew that the Contras were getting money from Los Angeles drug dealers. Webb, who subsequently resigned from the paper, said he was not "backing down from the central assertions of the story" (see Zoglin, 1997).[3] Under pressure from the Congressional Black Caucus and its chair Maxine Waters (who represents South Central Los Angeles) the CIA conducted its own investigation of the Webb allegations. Not surprisingly, the CIA found no evidence to support a CIA-drug connection. Indeed, the headline reporting on the CIA's investigation read "As Expected, CIA report denies drug-Contra link" (Weiner, 1998).[4]

Although the establishment press and most white political leaders dismissed the Webb story and rumors of a CIA conspiracy as paranoid conspiracism without merit, it was embraced—almost eagerly—by the black press and by most leaders of black America, including Maxine Waters of the Congressional Black Caucus; Joe Madison, a Washington, D.C., radio-talk-show host and a member of the NAACP's National Board; and Dick Gregory, the social activist. Madison and

Gregory engaged in hunger strikes and were arrested outside CIA headquarters while protesting.

The mainstream white view might be summed up by the reporting of the *Weekly Standard*, which headlined its account of the controversy about Webb's story "A Disgraceful Newspaper Expose and Its Fans" (Carlson, 1996). By contrast, the Nation of Islam's newspaper the *Final Call* titled its editorial on the subject, "The CIA Drug Lords" (*Final Call*, 1996).

The mainstream black view was expressed in *USA Today* by veteran columnist Barbara Reynolds (1996):

> But for the most part, the issue that feels like a dagger in the heart of African Americans is not a high priority among white power brokers. And like the O. J. Simpson trials, it exposes the deep gulf that separates the black experience from that of whites. As the CIA crack issue is ignored and true believers are dismissed as paranoid or conspiracy nuts, black indignation grows.

Given what Reynolds described as the "deep gulf" in opinion between black and white elites, we are not surprised to find that opinion at the mass level is similarly divided. We have four surveys in which this issue was raised: two conducted by the *New York Times*/CBS News six years prior to the Webb exposé and two conducted after the exposé, one by Southern Focus, and one by Scripps Howard at Ohio State University. The results are reported in table 5.1.

Whether conducted before or after the Webb exposé, the data displayed in the table shows a consistent race difference, either a gulf or a chasm. In the June 1990 *New York Times*/CBS News survey (devoted to race relations in New York City), 82% of whites but only 36% of blacks agreed that it was "certainly not true" that the government deliberately makes drugs available in black neighborhoods in order to harm blacks—a chasm of 46. Four years later, the *New York Times*/CBS News found a chasm of 52.

The publication of the Webb story may have had some impact in altering white opinion on this issue, although the results are ambiguous. The Southern Focus poll conducted in the spring of 1997 (more than six months after Webb's story) found that 64% of whites but only 6% of blacks were prepared to agree that it was "absolutely not true" that the government deliberately made drugs available in the black community. On the CIA connection explicitly, far more blacks (72%) than whites (43%) claimed to have heard of CIA involvement with crack cocaine. And blacks were more likely to think it true by a chasm of 57. Although the Scripps/ Howard survey shows a narrowing of this chasm to a gulf of 27, this may be a function of the differences in response wording ("very likely" or "somewhat likely" true compared to the more definite "absolutely true") and/or the sample or overall design and the purposes of the surveys.

Like many conspiracies and rumors, it probably will never be definitively known whether the CIA or other government agencies or their employees are or were

Table 5.1   Racial Differences in Opinion on Government Involvement in Drug Trafficking

	Blacks	Whites	Gulf/Chasm
Some people say the government deliberately makes sure that drugs are easily available in black neighborhoods in order to harm black people. Do you think that this is true, or that it might possibly be true, or that it is certainly not true?			
Certainly not true—June 1990[a]	36%	82%	Chasm—46
Certainly not true—February 1994[b]	29	81	Chasm—52
Absolutely not true—Spring 1997[c]	6	64	Chasm—58
Have you heard about the CIA being involved in the distribution of crack cocaine in this country?[d] (% responding yes)	72	43	Gulf—29
Some people say the CIA has been involved in importing cocaine for distribution in the black community. Do you think this is absolutely true, probably true, probably not true, or absolutely not true?[e] (% responding true)	73	16	Chasm—57
The CIA has deliberately allowed Central American drug dealers to sell cocaine to black kids in inner-city neighborhoods. How likely do you think this is? Very likely, somewhat likely, or not likely at all?[f] (% responding very or somewhat likely)	82	55	Gulf—27

[a]From *New York Times*/CBS-TV poll of race relations in New York City conducted June 1990.
[b]*New York Times*/CBS News nationwide poll on race relations in the United States, conducted February 1994. The question wording is the same as the June 1990 *Times*/CBS-TV poll.
[c]From nationwide poll conducted by Southern Focus in the spring of 1997. The question wording was the same as the *Times*/CBS poll, except *absolutely* was used rather than *certainly*.
[d]This item is from the Spring 1997 Southern Focus poll.
[e]This item is from the Spring 1997 Southern Focus poll.
[f]This item is from a poll conducted by Scripps Howard/Ohio University in the summer of 1997.

involved in some way with the widespread availability of drugs in black America. However, we would be loathe to agree that it is "definitely" or "absolutely" not true. There is, for example, some documentation or proof of CIA complicity in heroin smuggling in Europe after World War II and in Southeast Asia in the 1960s as part of strategies to destabilize radical and communist movements (McCoy, 1991; Scott and Marshall, 1991). In their thoroughly researched study, Scott and Marshall (1991: 302) concluded:

> The history of official toleration for or complicity with drug traffickers in Central America in the 1980s suggests the inadequacy of traditional "supply-side" or "de-

mand-side" drug strategies whose targets are remote from Washington. Chief among these targets have been the ethnic ghettos of America's inner cities (the demand side) and foreign peasants who grow cocoa plants or opium poppies (the supply side). Experience suggests instead that one of the first targets for an effective drug strategy should be Washington itself, and specifically its own support for corrupt, drug-linked forces in the name of anticommunism.

However, as with other conspiracisms against blacks examined in this chapter, whether one believes that the CIA or other government agencies are involved in the drug trade (or, more specifically, what separates black and white opinion whether elite or mass) is less about the probable truth or falsity of the allegations. Rather, the belief or disbelief is more likely structured by cultural differences and "group-serving" biases among both blacks and whites[5] (we discuss group-serving bias later in the chapter). We return to discussion of these aspects of race opinion differences after we analyze two other race conspiracy theories.

AIDS

During the early 1980s, acquired immune deficiency syndrome (AIDS) became the most widely discussed health problem in the world. When AIDS first emerged in the United States, it was considered primarily a disease of white homosexual or bisexual men. By the late 1980s, however, AIDS was becoming increasingly dominant among blacks, especially black women and children (Seltzer and Smith, 1988; McBride, 1991: 160). Whereas black men were more than two and a half times as likely to contract AIDS as white men, black women were an astonishing twelve times as likely to contract the disease as white women; and blacks constituted more than 50% of AIDS cases among children (McBride, 1991: 160).[6] Also, as AIDS became a prominent national issue in American and Western medical circles, the idea begin to circulate that the disease had its origins in the black republic of Haiti and in Africa, a view rejected by black scholars as racialist if not racist (see Katner and Pankey, 1989; Chirimula and Chirimula, 1987).

AIDS's rapid spread among blacks and its association in origins with African people fairly quickly led to rumors in the black community that the HIV virus that causes AIDS may have been deliberately created by the government to destroy black people (AIDS is also widespread in many parts of Africa). This rumor was quickly embraced by certain elements of the black nationalist community in the United States, especially the Nation of Islam and its leader Louis Farrakhan (Gardell, 1996: 324–38). As Abdul Alim Muhammad, the Nation's Minister of Health and a trained physician, frequently states in writings and lectures, "AIDS is part of a genocidal plot designed to wipe out the blacks of the world" (quoted in Gardell, 1996: 328).

How widespread among blacks is belief in this notion of AIDS as a conspiracy?

And how large is the expected race division? We were able to locate two survey items relevant to this question. The first was in the *New York Times*/CBS News survey on race relations conducted in New York City in June of 1990 and the second by Southern Focus in the spring of 1997. The results are reported in table 5.2.

In New York City, 95% of whites but 69% of blacks agreed that it was "certainly not true" that AIDS was deliberately created in a laboratory to infect black people (a gulf of 26). Many more blacks (31%) than whites (5%) said it was "true" or "might be possibly true" (also a gulf of 26). The Southern Focus poll posed three AIDS-related questions. On whether AIDS was caused by a manmade virus, 58% of blacks said "probably true" or "absolutely true," compared to 23% of whites (a gulf of 35). And in a slight variation on the *New York Times*/CBS News question, 60% of blacks but only 14% of whites agreed that, whatever its origins, the "government does not make a strong effort to combat AIDS because the government cares less about black people than whites"; a huge chasm of 46 is evident. A chasm almost as large divides the races on whether AIDS was being used as a plot to kill blacks, 62% compared to 21%. It is interesting to observe that in this 1997 poll a fifth (21%) of whites in this nationwide survey (compared to 5% in

Table 5.2   Racial Differences in Opinion on HIV-AIDS as a Conspiracy

	Blacks	*Whites*	*Gulf/Chasm*
Some people say that the virus which causes AIDS was deliberately created in a laboratory in order to infect black people. Do you think that this is true, or that it might be possibly true, or that it is certainly not true?			
Certainly not true—June 1990[a]	69%	95%	Gulf—26
Certainly not true—Spring 1997[b]	60	14	Chasm—46
Some people say that AIDS is a manmade virus. Do you think that this is absolutely true, probably true, probably not true, or absolutely not true?			
Probably true and absolutely true—Spring 1997[c]	58	23	Gulf—35
Some people say that HIV and AIDS are being used as part of a plot to deliberately kill African Americans. Do you think that this is absolutely true, probably true, probably not true, or absolutely not true?			
Probably true and absolutely true—Spring 1997[d]	62	21	Chasm—41

[a]*New York Times*/CBS-TV poll on race relations in New York City, June 1990.
[b]Southern Focus nationwide poll, Spring 1997. The question wording is identical to the *Times*/CBS poll except *absolutely* is used rather than *certainly*.
[c]Southern Focus poll.
[d]Southern Focus poll.

the New York City survey) are prepared to embrace AIDS conspiracism, although the wording of the question is somewhat different—"deliberately created . . . in order to infect" blacks rather "as part of a plot to deliberately kill" blacks.

What is one to make of this conspiracy theory and its acceptance by large numbers of blacks? In our view, this particular rumor is almost certainly not true. However, it is too easy to simply dismiss it as paranoid nonsense among blacks. African Americans may embrace this seemingly preposterous idea that the government would create or use a horrible disease to harm or to destroy its black citizens because many can quickly recall the infamous Tuskegee experiments, a racist project that denied treatment to black men with syphilis (Jones, 1982). The historical memory of Tuskegee creates skepticism about diseases and traditional American medicine, leading even sober scholars to see the current AIDS crisis among blacks as symptomatic of institutional racism in American medical science and its health care delivery system (see McBride, 1991; Holmes, Hodges, and Rich, 1989). Also, it is documented that the CIA and the military during the Cold War sometimes used poor black prisoners and mental patients in experiments with LSD and other drugs in order to develop some new incapacitating agents for purposes of warfare (see Lee and Shlain, 1992).

Conspiracies against Black Elected Officials

In the wake of the indictment in the late 1970s and the 1980s of a number of black elected leaders, rumors began to circulate in black leadership circles and at the mass level that black leaders were being deliberately targeted for investigation and prosecution by federal and state law enforcement officials. Of course, in many instances these rumors were advanced by people who had been themselves indicted, including Maryland State Senator Clarence Mitchell III and former Tennessee Congressman Harold Ford Sr.

It is difficult to document rumors of this sort (see Sawyer, 1977). Although the Congressional Black Caucus conducted informal hearings on whether there is any basis to the allegations, the truth is difficult to ascertain.[7] Known or not, the rumor is widely believed among blacks. Again, using the *New York Times*/CBS News poll, 83% of blacks agreed that it was true or might be true that the government deliberately singled out black elected officials to discredit them. And 37% of whites agreed, a fairly large proportion, but nevertheless a race chasm of 46.

Conspiracism and Blacks: A Note of Explanation

In their work on black-white differences in understanding the extent, causes, and remedies for racial inequality, Sigelman and Welch advanced the theory of "group-serving bias"—that individuals, when they can plausibly do so, attempt to explain their individual or their group's successes or failures in ways that cast themselves in a favorable light (1994: 96). They wrote:

Among blacks, a group-serving bias would be consistent with blaming whites or society in general for blacks' problems while crediting blacks for the progress they made in recent years. Among whites, a group-serving bias would be consistent with blaming blacks for their problems while crediting whites or society in general for the progress blacks have made in recent years. (1994: 97)

As a minority people who are disaffected and alienated and who have a long memory of victimization by whites, a group-serving bias is one way to explain the victimization of the black community by drugs and AIDS and the criminalization of their leaders. The alternative is to blame "the race"—to say that blacks themselves are to blame for the plague of AIDS, for crack use, and for miscreant leaders (a view advanced by some black conservative intellectuals, for example, Loury, 1985). This alternative is not an easy point of view to embrace, thus these problems must be the responsibility of continuing victimization by whites. And there are ample historical memories and experience to suggest that even the seemingly most outlandish behavior by whites might possibly be true.[8] As Turner put it in *I Heard It through The Grapevine*, these rumors may be a means for the "cultural body" to protect itself against subsequent infection.

Similarly, it would be difficult for the white majority to embrace the notion that the government it ostensibly controls could engage in such devilish, nefarious plots as deliberately using deadly viruses and drugs to destroy a people. Therefore, such rumors definitely must not be true—a group-serving bias that says blacks must be to blame for their own problems. Indeed, it is perhaps remarkable that in some cases, as much as a fourth of whites embrace some of these conspiracies.

If data permitted, we would like to know more about those blacks and whites who cross the color line to reject the group-serving bias. All we can say is that, in general, demographic variables such as gender, age, and education do not, for the most part, account for the intraracial differences.

If blacks' embrace of antiblack conspiracies (compared to whites) is largely or even significantly due to group-serving bias rather than to a more general disposition to embrace conspiracy theories—whether rationally based ones or those with scant credibility—then we would expect fewer or no chasms and few gaps and gulfs between the races when nonrace specific conspiracies are involved.

THE ASSASSINATION OF PRESIDENT KENNEDY AND OTHER CONSPIRACY THEORIES

The murder of President John F. Kennedy in 1963 is perhaps the most widely believed conspiracy in recent U.S. history. Indeed, the Kennedy assassination conspiracism is a cottage industry that started as soon as the official report of the government's investigative commission was released. This commission, headed by Chief Justice Earl Warren, found that Lee Harvey Oswald acted alone in murdering the president. This finding was almost immediately challenged by skeptics (see Epstein, 1966; Lane, 1966), and subsequently there have been hundreds of books and articles, scores of movies and docudramas, countless television investigative reports, and a congressional investigation suggesting that the president's death was part of a conspiracy.

Why the fascination with the Kennedy assassination? In the aftermath of the murder of President Abraham Lincoln, there were also conspiracy rumors. So, in a sense, the Kennedy case is not without precedent. However, the dramatic manner in which Kennedy was killed, the capturing of the event in living color on video, the three-day televising of his funeral, and then the televised murder of the accused assassin Oswald have all contributed to Kennedy conspiracism. Also, the elaborate Camelot myth created and sustained by the Kennedy family created a legacy of a heroic young leader, taken away on the verge of greatness.

The image of Kennedy as the fallen hero is especially powerful in the African American community because he was the first American president, albeit reluctantly, to unambiguously embrace the cause of racial equality and civil rights as morally and constitutionally imperative. At the time of his murder in broad daylight in a downtown southern city, Kennedy was pushing for passage of what would become the Civil Rights Act of 1964. As a result, more than thirty years after his death, one finds in many African American homes portraits of the president often along with those of Jesus and Martin Luther King Jr. Thus, the idea of a conspiracy to kill Kennedy might have special allure in the black community.

The data displayed in table 5.3 show that it does, but not by very much. First, most blacks (93%) and whites (85%) reject the official judgment that Oswald acted alone. Virtually all black respondents think there was an official coverup of the assassination (97%, compared to 86% of whites), but here there is only a modest race gap. Nearly three-fourths of blacks compared to a little more than half of whites believe it is likely that officials in the federal government were directly responsible for the murder of the president, a gulf of 20.

In terms of theories of who might have been involved in the conspiracy, majorities of both blacks and whites point the finger at the CIA; however, there is a race gap of 15 (84% of blacks, 69% of whites). The races do not differ on the possibility of Mafia involvement (about half think so), but whites are more likely than blacks to suspect Cuban or Soviet involvement. The differences here, however, are modest gaps.

The data on the Kennedy assassination show that blacks are a bit more likely to embrace conspiracism; but given Kennedy's mythic link with the cause of civil rights, in some ways this might be viewed indirectly as a group-serving bias.

It is widely believed among blacks that there were also conspiracies to kill not only President Kennedy but also the two major black leaders of the 1960s, Martin

Table 5.3   Racial Differences in Opinion on the Assassination of President Kennedy*

	Blacks	Whites	Gap/Gulf
Did Oswald act alone, or do you think others were involved? (% saying others involved)	93%	85%	—
Do you think there was an official cover-up to keep the public from learning the truth about the Kennedy assassination? (% saying yes)	97	86	Gap—11
There have been many theories about who was involved in the assassination. I'd like to know if you think any of the following groups were involved in assassination. (% saying involved)			
Mafia	49	53	—
CIA	84	69	Gap—15
Cubans	20	36	Gap—16
Soviet Union	12	21	Gap—
Here are several serious accusations that some people have made against the federal government in recent years. Please tell me if you think each of these is very likely, somewhat likely, somewhat unlikely.			
Officials in the federal government were directly responsible for the assassination of President Kennedy. (% saying likely)	72	52	Gulf—20

*The first three questions are from a *New York Times*/CBS News poll conducted in October 1993. The last item is from the Scripps Howard/Ohio University poll conducted in the summer of 1997.

Luther King Jr. and Malcolm X. (Indeed, at this first writing in the summer of 1998—thirty years after the murder—the King family is pressing the president and the Justice Department to appoint a commission to investigate Dr. King's assassination.)[9] We were not able to locate any polls or surveys dealing with the murder of Malcolm X; however, as we neared completion of this work, a CBS News telephone survey of 782 adults on the King assassination was released. It found that 66% of whites and nearly all blacks (94%) believed that the accused assassin, James Earl Ray, did not act alone but rather as part of a conspiracy to murder Dr. King. Although there is a race gulf of 28, it is striking that two-thirds of whites reject the official explanation of King's death. Commenting on the CBS News poll, Samuel Yette, a black columnist, wrote, "There is enough sickening evidence of a conspiracy to go around" (Yette, 1998). The CBS News poll did not ask respondents who might have been involved in King's murder. Yette, however, included the U.S. Army, the FBI, and even members of King's own inner circle as possible culprits.

Other Conspiracies

The data in table 5.4 show that there is a tendency among blacks to embrace conspiracism, even when they are not related to race, either directly or indirectly. In the several cases displayed in table 5.4—whether President Franklin Roosevelt knew in advance of the Japanese attack on Pearl Harbor, whether the FBI might have deliberately set the Waco, Texas, fire in 1993, whether the U.S. Navy might have deliberately or accidentally shot down TWA flight 800, and whether the government might have bombed the Oklahoma City federal building in 1995— blacks are more likely to believe in the possibility of conspiracy. Except for the Oklahoma City bombing, for which 24% of blacks and 8% of whites embrace conspiracism, majorities or near majorities of both races are willing to embrace

Table 5.4   Racial Differences in Opinion on Selected Conspiracy Theories involving the Federal Government[*]

	Likely		
	Blacks	*Whites*	*Gap*
President Roosevelt knew in advance that the Japanese were going to attack Pearl Harbor, but he did not warn our troops because he wanted to get the United States involved in World War II. Do you think this is likely or not?	65%	47%	18
The FBI deliberately set fires that destroyed the Branch Davidian Compound in Waco, Texas, in 1993.[**]	55	44	11
The U.S. Navy, either by accident or on purpose, shot down TWA passenger flight 800 near New York City last year [1996] and is covering up what it did.	57	43	14

	Possibly True		
	Blacks	*Whites*	*Gap*
Some people have said that the government might have bombed the federal building in Oklahoma City itself in order to blame extremist groups. Do you think this might possibly be true or that it is almost certainly not true?	24%	8%	16

[*]These four question are from the Scripps Howard/Ohio University poll, Summer 1997.
[**]The Branch Davidian is a religious sect. It was accused by the federal government of illegal possession of firearms. After a several-week standoff between the sect and federal authorities, the group's compound was attacked and subsequently burned to the ground, killing scores of men, women, and children. The FBI claimed the fire was unanticipated (see Wright, 1995).

the possibility of conspiracies. It appears, therefore, that race-specific distrust of the government among blacks carries over to a belief in conspiracies in general. However, the differences between blacks and whites on these conspiracies are modest gaps rather than gulfs or chasms, suggesting that among all Americans there is an extraordinary degree of distrust of the government.

The Paranormal

Does the belief in plausibly possible but incredible government conspiracies translate into or relate to belief in the paranormal—phenomena not rationally or scientifically demonstrable? Apparently not (see table 5.5). Although blacks are somewhat more likely than whites to believe in heaven, hell, and angels—gaps of 11 to 19—this probably is a function of their religiosity and biblical literalism. On other paranormal—belief in UFOs, clairvoyance, astrology, reincarnation— there are small racial differences (whites are more likely to believe in UFOs).[10]

Table 5.5 Racial Differences in Attitudes toward the Paranormal*

	% Real		
	Blacks	Whites	Gap
Do you believe heaven is a real place or not?	94%	83%	11
Do you believe hell is real?	82	68	14
Do you believe angels are real?	93	74	19
Do you believe UFOs are real?	57	65	—
	% Yes		
	Blacks	Whites	Gap
Do you believe in clairvoyance, that is, the power of the mind to know the past and predict the future?	56%	53%	—
Do you believe in astrology, that the position of the stars and planets can affect people's lives?	58	45	13
Do you believe in reincarnation, that is, rebirth of the soul in a new body after birth?	49	43	—

*The first four items are from a *Washington Post*/ABC News poll, May 1994. The last three are from a Gallup Poll, September 1996.

CONCLUSION

African Americans are more likely to distrust and to be suspicious of the government, believing that it might engage in the most incredible, criminal conspiracies against them as a people and against the American people in general. African American history, culture, and memory provide some basis for understanding this phenomenon among blacks. But even among whites, there is an extremely high level of distrust and suspiciousness about the motives of government—nearly 70% believing, for example, that the CIA might have been involved in a plot to kill the president of the United States or that the government deliberately set fire to a religious sect's building in Texas killing more than seventy people or that it is covering up its involvement of the killing of more than two hundred people on a civilian aircraft. This is extraordinary, in some ways more so than black opinion. We know that neither white nor black conspiracy opinion is much affected by gender, age, or education, suggesting that it is a cultural phenemenon. However, we know little else.

Most of the academic studies of conspiracism deal with whites, focusing on right-wing extremism (see Lipset and Raab, 1978; Curry, 1972; Johnson, 1983). In his classic study of the paranoid as a persistent phenomenon in American politics, Hofstader (1979) referred in passing to the Nation of Islam, but only to make the point that paranoid tendencies exist among both blacks and whites[11]—the major focus of his work was on the white right wing. Even today, most of the serious work on conspiracism focuses on whites and the right wing, including for the most part Pipes's (1997) recent book.[12]

Pipes identified conspiracism among whites with what he called the "hard right." Unfortunately, Pipes offered little statistical data on the size of this group. The data presented in this chapter suggest that it is quite large—perhaps as large as one-third of the population. Our findings are consistent with other studies of right-wing extremist politics. Hoy, for example, wrote that "roughly one-third of white Americans feel that violence against the federal government will eventually prove necessary to save the 'true American way of life'" and that "these people, who love America . . . feel betrayed by a system they see as growing more alien" (1992: 91). Similarly, Warren (1976) identified a category of "Middle American Radicals" as constituting 31% of the white population. This group identified minorities, radicals, the federal government, the media, and big business as enemies of traditional American values.

Walters (1999) identified these Americans as "white nationalists." And, like extreme or radical black nationalists, a minority of white nationalists favor a separate white nation. Since 1992, polls conducted by Southern Focus at the University of North Carolina have shown between 8% and 16% of white Southerners, and up to 9% of nonsouthern whites supporting the establishment of a white nation in the old Confederacy (Breed, 1999).[13]

We conclude that much more attention should be given by scholars in their research and by journalists in their reporting to conspiracism and other forms of the paranoid in contemporary American politics, among both blacks and whites. But perhaps this attention should be paid more to whites than to blacks because among blacks conspiracism may represent little more than a benign cultural adaptation, whereas among whites it may lead individuals and groups to engage in paranoid, conspiratorial violence.[14]

NOTES

1. Gibbs developed these categories of conspiracy myths and motifs in her book that examined the O. J. Simpson and Rodney King cases.

2. On the streets of South Central Los Angeles, the CIA is sometimes referred to as the "Crack Importation Agency."

3. Webb subsequently (1998) wrote a book detailing his investigative report, the subsequent controversy, and his continued assertion of the story's basic accuracy.

4. Citing confidentiality in investigative procedures, the CIA and the Justice Department refused to release the full text of the report.

5. In general, on this and other race conspiracies, there are hardly any within-group differences—opinions among both blacks and whites tend to be relatively homogeneous with few differences in terms of gender, age, or education, although among blacks men and the college educated are more likely to believe in government involvement in drug trafficking.

6. In the most recent data, estimates are that 57% of all new HIV cases are black—63% of those cases are people 18 to 24 and 57% of the cases are women (see Stolberg, 1998).

7. Commentators noted that four of Clinton's six black cabinet members were targeted for criminal investigations, and rumors persist that one of them—Ronald Brown, the secretary of commerce—was murdered in the crash of a military aircraft in Europe.

The death of Secretary Brown is a recent case that illuminates very well the nature of modern conspiracism. Within days of his death, one of us (Smith) began to hear rumors of Brown's murder. Weeks later, an obscure right-wing Pittsburgh newspaper published a story claiming that one of the pathologists who examined Brown's body saw what appeared to be a bullet hole in Brown's skull but was denied the right to conduct an autopsy. This story was largely ignored by the mainstream press; however, it was picked up by the Associated Press and given some exposure. More exposure was provided by BET (Black Entertainment Television), which interviewed the reporter on its nightly nationally televised program, leading to calls for the exhumation of the body. The rejection of these calls by the government and the Brown family was then cited as evidence of a plot to cover up the conspiracy to murder Brown. Later, in the summer of 1998 (Brown was killed in 1996), a friend of Smith's who dabbles in the stock market received a pamphlet from an outfit called "The Wall Street Underground," edited by Nicholas A. Guarino. The pamphlet was a facsimile of an official congressional report, with no date; it read "MURDER IN THE FIRST DEGREE (in bold red type): AN INTERIM REPORT ON THE DEATH OF COMMERCE SECRETARY RON BROWN AND 34 OTHER UNITED STATES CITIZENS—CONCLUDING REPORT DATE CONTINGENT UPON HEARINGS IN HOUSE COMMITTEE ON NATIONAL SECURITY AND SENATE COMMITTEE ON GOVERNMENT AFFAIRS (PERMANENT SUBCOMMITTEE INVESTIGATIONS), TOP SECRET U.S. GOVERNMENT CLASSIFIED INFORMATION, LEAKED 5/14/96 BY MILITARY INFORMANT EYE THREE, PRIVATE REPORT, NOT PRINTED AT GOVERNMENT EXPENSE. NOT AUTHORIZED BY ANY AGENCY OF THE FEDERAL GOVERNMENT." Unlike the story in the Pittsburgh paper, this document claimed that Brown was not shot but that his U.S. Air Force plane was deliberately crashed into a mountain. Why? Because Brown was about to be indicted and had warned Clinton that he would bring the president down with him, by revealing incriminating information. Clinton then ordered the destruction of Brown's plane, which carried thirty-three other persons. The document claimed that these deaths brought to "56 Clinton dead." Brief summaries of these deaths were then provided.

Smith's friend said he found the report on Brown's death credible until he read the bogus investment advice also included in it.

8.   As we were near completing this manuscript, a new book (Case 1998) appeared that claimed that in 1943 the U.S. Army, after an altercation between black and white troops at Camp Van Dorin, Mississippi, machine gunned to death more than 1200 black soldiers, loaded them in boxcars, and buried them in a mass grave. (The families were told the men were killed in action in the Pacific theater.) Immediatelly, the NAACP called for an investigation. Sixteen months later the Army completed its investigation, having found that the report of the massacre was false and noting that it had been unable to locate a mass grave and that it had accounted for every man who served in the unit that allegedly suffered the atrocity. The NAACP, however, rejected the Army's findings and called for an independent review by the Justice Department, implying the possibility of an Army cover-up. Reflecting on this case, Professor John Sibley Butler of the University of Texas at Austin said, "This does not tell us anything about the history of blacks in America because there is no proof that it happened, but it does reveal something interesting about the way people see that history. So many bad things happened to black soldiers during that time period that something like this supposed slaughter could have happened; and because of that, people can put aside the question of whether or not there is evidence and simply believe that it did happen" (see Suro and Fletcher, 1999).

9.   In a rather bizarre twist, the King family sued Loyd Jowers, a retired Memphis businessman who claimed several years ago that he paid someone other than James Earl Ray (the confessed assassin) to kill King. The King family was represented in the suit by William Pepper, the attorney for Ray. After about three hours of deliberations, a jury of six blacks and six whites returned a verdict finding that there was a conspiracy to murder King and awarded the King family $100 in damages. The King family eagerly embraced the jury's verdict as vindication of their long-held view of conspiracism (*Jet*, December 27, 1999b), but most authorities on the King assassination dismissed the verdict as substantively irrelevant because it produced little new documentary evidence.

10.   Seventeen percent of whites and 18% of blacks report regularly reading an astrology column.

11.   Hofstader identified six components of the paranoid tradition in American politics. Apart from conspiracism, they are militancy, the identification of enemies, faith in redemption, ambivalence toward intellectuals, and an episodic character.

12.   Although polemical and written with evident ill will, Singh's book (1997) is an interesting attempt to locate Farrakhan in Hofstader's paranoid tradition.

13.   Organizers of a group called the Southern Party in 1999 registered with the Federal Election Commission and with the secretaries of state of several southern states. The party claims that its short-term goal is to elect members to state and local office, but its long-term objectives are to send enough party members to Congress to push for a separate southern nation (see Breed, 1999).

14.   The most infamous example of this in recent years is the bombing of the Oklahoma City federal building in 1995. However, as this book is first written, the media is filled with assorted stories of the killing of a black man and an Asian American man and of an assault on two orthodox Jews in suburban Chicago by twenty-one-year-old Benjamin Smith. Smith (who subsequently committed suicide) was a member of the World Church of the Creator, a white supremacist organization based in East Peoria, Illinois (Irvine, 1999).

6

Crimes and Punishments: An Overview of Race Opinion Differences

We conclude this inquiry into race differences in attitudes and opinions where it began, with the O. J. Simpson case. As we indicated at the outset, the inspiration for writing this book was the controversy surrounding the arrest, trial, and acquittal of Simpson for the murder of his wife, Nicole, and Ronald Goldman. A simple murder case, yet not so simple given the enormous controversy it generated and its reflection of the chasm between the races on a range of historically divisive issues—issues involving race and sex, gender and sexuality, celebrity and status, race and racism, and race and community. However, at its beginning and at its end, the Simpson controversy was about crime and punishment and race and justice in the United States.

Crime and punishment in the United States, as we argue later in the chapter, is an area of American life marked historically by the most egregious of racist practices, racist practices that persist to the present day. The Simpson case and the chasm in race opinion that it demonstrated can only be understood in the context of this history of institutional racism in crime and punishment in the United States.

To provide context beyond history, we also examine three other cases of crime and punishment. The first case involves the allegation of a brutal attack on a young black woman, Tawana Brawley, by New York police officers. Although Brawley's story was apparently false, her saga is illustrative of the deep divisions between blacks and whites on the police and on crime and punishment in the United States.

The second case goes beyond mere crime and punishment and raises significant political questions about the relationship between blacks and whites. In the
aftermath of the acquittal of the Los Angeles police offices who beat Rodney King,
the black and Latino communities erupted in riotous rebellion, the first major urban
revolt in a decade. The L.A. riots illustrated another dynamic of race opinion.
Whereas blacks and whites tended to agree in opinion on the verdict, opinion
diverged in opinion about the riots.

The third case involves District of Columbia Mayor Marion Barry. In the aftermath of the arrest, trial, conviction, and jailing of Barry, to the astonishment of
most Americans, Barry returned to be reelected first to the city's Council and then
as mayor. Opinion differences between blacks and whites in Washington diverged
so sharply on this phenomenon that it probably has no precedent in race opinion
surveys. Indeed, regarding Barry's reelection as mayor, the opinion differences
are so large that one might label it a "canyon" rather than a chasm.

Taken together, these four cases—O. J. Simpson, Tawana Brawley, Rodney
King, and Marion Barry—provide different contexts (national opinions in the case
of Simpson and King, local with Barry and Brawley) over a time period of almost
a decade to study the dynamic character of race opinion. Although there have been
other studies of these cases—especially Simpson and King—this is the first analysis
that makes use of the extensive available survey data.

AN OVERVIEW OF RACE OPINION DIFFERENCES

Before examining in detail the four cases, we present a summary of racial differences in attitudes toward them, comparing opinion differences in the first surveys
taken about the controversies. Subsequently, we examine how opinion differences
changed over time; but first we wish to present a snapshot of how blacks and
whites viewed the controversies at their beginnings. In table 6.1, we display data
on the Simpson, Brawley, Barry, and King cases. Although the Simpson case was
to become emblematic of deep racial divisions in the country, at the outset, opinion differences between the races were modest—gaps and gulfs rather than chasms.
There was no significant difference between blacks and whites on whether Simpson
could get a fair trial. Whites, however, were more likely than blacks to agree with
the outcome of the preliminary hearing in which a judge (an African American
woman) found there was sufficient evidence to bound Simpson over for trial—
89% versus 66%. And although the difference is a modest gap, 36% of whites
and 19% of blacks agreed that Simpson was probably guilty.

In the Brawley case there was a gulf of 35 between the races. Whereas 50% of
blacks agreed that Brawley was probably lying, this was the view of 85% of whites.

The Barry case at the outset evinced a near chasm. Respondents were asked
after Barry's arrest whether the government was out to get Barry or alternatively

Table 6.1 Summary, Overview of Racial Differences in Opinion on the Brawley, Barry, Simpson, and King Cases (% Agreeing)

	Blacks	Whites	Gap	Gulf	Chasm
Simpson					
Fair trial is possible	52%	50%	—		
Agree with decision of preliminary hearing	66	89		23	
Simpson probably guilty	19	36	17		
Brawley					
Brawley probably lying	50	85		35	
Barry					
Barry to blame for his arrest	26	65		39	
Barry should resign	54	77		23	
Barry should run again for mayor	30	4		26	
Would vote for Barry if he ran	46	5			41
King					
Verdict wrong	100	93	—		
Verdict shows blacks can't get justice	81	27			54
Videotape enough evidence for conviction	92	54		38	

Source: In each of the cases, these results are from the first surveys conducted on the cases. The Brawley survey was conducted by the *New York Times*/CBS News in June 1988; the Barry survey was conducted by the *Washington Post* in February 1990; the Simpson poll was conducted by the *New York Times*/CBS News in June 1994; and the King poll was conducted by the *Washington Post* in April 1992.

was Barry to blame for his predicament. Although not mutually exclusive alternatives (that is, both could be true in that the government was out to get Barry and he was to blame for engaging in behavior that allowed the government to indeed get him), respondents did tend to choose one of the alternatives—65% of whites but only 26% of blacks blamed Barry. This near chasm is not reflected in opinion on whether Barry should resign—77% of whites thought he should, compared to 54% of blacks, a gulf of 23. Finally, in this first postarrest poll, 30% of blacks said Barry should seek reelection as mayor and 46% indicated that they would vote for him if he did. By contrast, an insignificant 4% and 5% of whites held similar views. Thus, at the outset of the Barry controversy, there was already considerable support in the black community to reelect Barry, in spite of his illicit and illegal behavior.

Finally, in the Rodney King case, 100% of black respondents agreed that the verdict of not guilty for the police officers was wrong but so did 90% of whites—

no significant race differences here. However, a gulf and a chasm emerge on the implications of the verdict. Of blacks, 92% thought the videotaped beating of King was enough to warrant conviction, but only slightly more than half of whites agreed, a gulf of 38. And 81% of blacks thought the verdict indicated that blacks could not get justice in the United States, compared to only 27% of whites, a huge chasm of 54.

Although both blacks and whites thought the verdict in the King case was a miscarriage of justice, whites apparently saw the verdict as an aberration, an isolated incident, whereas blacks apparently saw the verdict as systemic, an institutionalized practice of injustice toward blacks. A glance at the history of blacks in the American criminal justice system and at their current predicament in this system will go a long way toward explaining this chasm in opinion on the implications of the King verdict, as well as the differences between the races on the other three cases.

RACISM IN CRIME AND PUNISHMENT: HISTORICAL BACKGROUND AND CONTEMPORARY CIRCUMSTANCES

In probably no area of American life—not voting, officeholding, education, health, housing, or employment—have African Americans suffered racist oppression to a greater extent than in the area of crime and punishment, involving as it does the loss of life and liberty. Randall Kennedy's *Race, Crime, and Law* (1997) and David Cole's *No Equal Justice: Race and Class in the American Criminal Justice System* (1999) are the most recent of the books documenting the systematic history of racism in America's judicial system, a history that leads many blacks to view the legal system with suspicion and distrust, resulting in what Kennedy calls a "crisis of legitimacy," (On the history of racism in the legal system, see also Bell, 1980.)

The Kennedy, the Cole, and related studies have shown that historically blacks have had disproportionately high crime rates; that black communities have not received adequate police protection; that blacks have been disproportionately victimized by crime; that police officers have consistently engaged in patterns of misconduct, maltreatment, brutality, and murder; that blacks have not received "due process" or fair trials; and that blacks have been punished much more severely for comparable crimes than whites (see also Jaynes and Williams, 1989: chap. 9). Also, in the twentieth century, African American political leaders were victimized by a historic pattern of political surveillance, provocations, and repression by police, intelligence, and military authorities (O'Reilly, 1994; Tompkins, 1993).

These historical patterns manifest themselves in present-day circumstances. First, blacks continue to exhibit disproportionately high rates of crime and to be disproportionately victims of crime. In any given year, the FBI Uniform Crime Reports indicate that although about 12% of the population is African American, they are arrested for about 40% of the murders, rapes, and other violent crimes. And most of the people killed, raped, and assaulted by blacks are other blacks. Thus, as Jaynes and Williams wrote, "During all periods for which systematic data are available, blacks have been overrepresented both as victims and [as] offenders" (1989: 455).

In many parts of the country, black communities still receive inadequate police services and protection. And blacks continue to be mistreated, brutalized, beaten, and killed by the police. In the aftermath of the Rodney King beating, the NAACP in collaboration with the Harvard Law School Criminal Justice Institute and the Monroe Trotter Institute of the University of Massachusetts conducted a study of police–community relations in black America. The report concluded: "The beating of Rodney King is part of a long and shameful history of racially motivated brutality and degradation that continues to find expression in powerful places" (quoted in Ogletree, 1995: 261).[1] Walters (1987: 14) cited figures from the Police Foundation that show that during the 1980s 78% of those killed and 80% of those nonfatally shot were minorities. Apparently, the police use of deadly force increased in the 1980s, up 43% in 1983 from 1980. Walters noted that the police shootings were rarely prosecuted and wrote: "The only factors which appeared to restrain the growth of such official, racially motivated violence was not the criminal justice system itself, but the election of sensitive black mayors who initiated new policies for the use of deadly force" (1987: 14).

Allegations of abuse or misconduct by police or other law enforcement agencies are rarely prosecuted by the Justice Department. The Associated Press (AP) analyzed computer records of all 1.4 million cases considered by the Justice Department between 1992 and 1996 and reviewed other department documents obtained through the Freedom of Information Act. The AP found that in 96% of the roughly 2,000 civil rights criminal cases referred each year, federal prosecutors took no action. This compares to prosecutions in 90% of immigration cases referred and 75% of drug cases. Overall, the Justice Department prosecutes in about half of all criminal matters referred to it, leading the AP to conclude that "civil rights crimes are the department's lowest prosecutorial priority" (Associated Press, 1999).[2]

After the Rodney King verdict, a 1993 study of reports of police brutality in fifteen major daily newspapers between January 1990 and May 1992 found that the majority of the victims of police brutality were black. Of 131 such victims reported during this period, 87% were black, 10% were Latino, and 3% were white. By contrast, 93% of the officers involved were white, suggesting a national pattern of misconduct by white police officers toward black citizens (Lersch, 1993).

Congressman John Conyers, the senior black on the House Judiciary Committee, estimated that 72% of the car drivers stopped by the police are black. Their offense of "DWB"—driving while black—is an offense from which no black is immune. As Congressman Conyers remarked on the House floor: "There are virtually no African American males—including Congressmen, actors, athletes, and office workers—who have not been stopped at one time or another for an alleged traffic violation, namely driving while black" (quoted in Jackson, 1998).[3] According to a 1999 Gallup poll (of 2,006 Americans, including 1,001 blacks and 934 whites), 56% of whites and 77% of blacks believe that "racial profiling" is widespread (that is, that police officers stop motorists of certain racial or ethnic groups because they believe these groups are more likely to commit certain types of crimes), a gulf of 27. Moreover, 57% of black respondents indicated that they believe they had been stopped by the police "just because of their race," a figure that rises to 72% among blacks ages 18 to 34 (see Lester, 1999).

As was the case with the Los Angeles riots of 1992, most of the major riots of the 1960s were touched off by encounters with the police. The 1969 *Report of the National Advisory Commission on Civil Disorders* (the so-called Kerner Report, after the Illinois governor who chaired the commission) found that police misconduct was the leading grievance of urban blacks against local authorities and frequently a precipitant cause of the riots (U.S. National Advisory Commission, 1968). The commission found that grievances against the police were greater in intensity than was concern about discrimination in housing, employment, or education. Thus, the response of the Los Angeles black community to the King verdict was historically predictable (on black-white police relations in Los Angeles in the 1980s, see Davis, 1990).

And blacks continue to be punished in a disproportionately harsh manner, compared to whites and to other minorities. Jaynes and Williams (1989: 497) wrote: "Historically discrimination against blacks in arrests and sentencing was ubiquitous." It remains so in present circumstances. Ogletree wrote: "Prosecutors are more likely to pursue full prosecutions, file more severe charges, and seek more stringent penalties in cases involving minority defendants, particularly where the victims are white" (1995: 254).

The United States imprisons more people than any other country in the world except Russia—in 1998 about two million people, almost twice the number in 1985 (Gearan, 1999). Nearly 40% of these people are African Americans. Furthermore, in 1995 more than 32% of young black men (20–29-year-olds) were in jail or prison or were on parole or probation, compared to only 7% of young white men. Indeed, astonishingly, the percentage of young black women in jail (5%) is almost as large as that for white men (7%) (only 1.5% of white women are jailed) (Mauer, 1995). Some of this disproportionately high rate of black incarceration is due to the fact that young black men who are poor commit more crimes than whites, but perhaps equally important is racial discrimination in the criminal justice system and unfairness in the punishment for use of illegal drugs. In 1995, the *Nashville Tennessean* (Frank, 1995) analyzed all 1992–1993 convictions in all federal district courts in the United States. The study found that black criminals' sentences were up to 40% longer than those of white criminals in some courts and that blacks are less likely than whites to get a break on their sentences. This racial disparity existed in all parts of the country, but it is interesting that it was highest in the West (California) and lowest in the South. And it was only a black–white disparity, as Hispanics received the same sentences for the same crime as whites (there were too few Asians to make a comparison) (see Frank, 1995).

Adding to this disparity in crime and punishment is the so-called war on drugs. Under federal law, a person convicted of selling 5 grams of crack cocaine receives a mandatory five years in prison; but if the illegal substance is *powdered* cocaine, a person would have to sell 250 grams to get a five-year sentence (a 100-to-1 ratio). Ninety percent of the people convicted of selling crack cocaine are black; 90% of those convicted of selling powdered cocaine are white. Thus, blacks are given sentences five times as great as whites because their illegal drug of choice is crack rather than powdered cocaine. These racial sentencing disparities have been challenged and upheld in the federal courts; and shortly after the Million Man March on October 16, 1995, the House of Representatives voted down a Congressional Black Caucus bill that would have equalized sentences for powdered and crack cocaine.

Finally, there is clear and convincing statistical evidence that the death penalty is imposed in a racially discriminatory manner. In *McClesky v. Kemp*,[4] the Supreme Court was presented with statistical proof that race influences death sentencing. Professor David Baldus and his colleagues used the state of Georgia as a case study, analyzing more than two thousand murders in the state during the 1970s. Among other things, Baldus found that a black was about twenty-two times as likely to be sentenced to die for killing a white than for killing a black. On hearing this evidence, Justice Lewis Powell, writing for the Court's majority to uphold the Georgia death penalty law, said the evidence at best indicated "a statistical discrepancy that correlates with race" and that "apparent disparities in sentencing are an inevitable part of criminal justice"; and to rule in favor of the black defendant would mean "we would soon be faced with similar claims as to other types of penalty." In other words, Justice Powell agreed that perhaps there is racial discrimination in imposition of the death penalty but, alas, that there is discrimination in all types of sentencing. Thus, to strike down the death penalty as discriminatory would mean that sentencing in all types of cases could be challenged (on the McClesky case, see Kennedy, 1988).

Awareness of this history and circumstances of the relationship of African Americans to the legal system in the United States is necessary if one is to appreciate the extent of the racial differences in opinions on the Brawley, Simpson, Barry, and King cases. Summing up the injustices of the American system of justice in the late 1960s, Knowles and Prewitt (1969: 66) wrote: "In the typical case, the black person suspected of a crime is arrested by a white police officer, brought to face a white judge, district attorney, and jury in a courtroom where the proceedings are recorded by white clerks, and upon conviction sent to a prison where the only black employees are custodians." Although some progress has been made in integration of blacks into the criminal justice system since the 1960s, this is still how the criminal justice system is and appears to blacks.

The cases we examine in this chapter reveal the extent to which blacks and whites differ in their views of justice in America, particularly on whether the legacy of racist oppression and repression persists.

THE TAWANA BRAWLEY CASE

On the Saturday after Thanksgiving in 1987, Tawana Brawley, then a fifteen-year-old African American, was found in a plastic bag, smeared with feces, her hair yanked out, with "KKK" scrawled on her body. Brawley claimed that she had been kidnapped on the previous Wednesday near a friend's home in Newburgh, New York (about 50 miles north of New York City), and raped by a gang of four white men. She also claimed that one or more of the men were wearing police uniforms. New York City and the nation recoiled in horror at this young girl's story of police brutality. The case became a celebrated cause in New York. On the advice of activist minister Reverend Al Sharpton and attorneys C. Vernon Mason and Alton Maddox, Brawley and her family refused to cooperate with local authorities and the state attorney general, claiming they were biased. Instead, Sharpton and the lawyers called on Governor Mario Cuomo to appoint a special, independent prosecutor. Cuomo refused, and Brawley continued to fail to cooperate with the investigation.

For nearly a year, the controversy continued, with widespread coverage in the New York City and national media. Sharpton, Mason, and Maddox assumed public roles after the incident, making unsubstantiated allegations that Brawley "had been raped and sodomized by a gang of white men and left to die, they said they knew [sic]; one of her assailants had urinated in her mouth and medical tests had detected five types of semen on her body. . . . They described Tawana's assailants first as a 'pack of Ku Klux Klansmen'; then as a racist cult inside the Dutchess County Sheriff's office that was connected to the Irish Republican Army; and finally as a group of white men, including a part-time cop, an assistant prosecutor, and a state trooper, all of whom they named" (Taibi and Sims-Phillips, 1989: xii).

In addition to extensive coverage in the New York City media, the Brawley case received widespread coverage in the national and African American media. As a result, Brawley received support from such disparate figures as entertainer Bill Cosby, boxing promoter Don King, boxer Mike Tyson, and Minister Louis Farrakhan.

Nine months after the incident, a New York grand jury amassed substantial evidence that Brawley's assault story was a hoax—the desperate story of a young girl trying to escape punishment by someone she knew (presumably because she had been away from home without the permission of relatives). The grand jury's conclusion is supported by the only book-length account of the incident, written by two reporters (one black, one white) who covered the story for WCBS-TV news in New York (see Taibi and Sims-Phillips, 1989), and by an extensive investigative report by Les Payne, the veteran African American journalist (1989).

The *New York Times* and WCBS television conducted one survey that tapped opinion on the Brawley case. This survey was part of a series the *Times* and WCBS conducted on race relations in New York City.[5] Thus, we are able to place opinions on the Brawley case in the larger context of race relations in New York.

The survey was administered in June 1988 during the peak of the controversy about the incident. Table 6.2 displays attitudes on Brawley's allegations and opinions on her principal advisers and spokespersons, Sharpton, Mason, and Maddox. Only 3% of whites thought Brawley was telling the truth compared to 27% of blacks. The overwhelming majority of whites (85%) thought she was lying, compared to 51% of blacks, a gulf of 34. Very few black or white New Yorkers had favorable opinions of Sharpton, Mason, and Maddox, although among whites essentially no one viewed them favorably. Yet, gulfs in the 25–30 range are observed. For example, 84% of whites viewed Sharpton unfavorably compared to 55% of blacks.

Putting the Brawley opinion in the larger context of race relations in New York City, since the election of Edward Koch as mayor in 1977, relations between blacks and whites were thought to be strained. Koch's conservative reform administra-

Table 6.2 Racial Differences in Opinion on Tawana Brawley and Her Principal Advisers/ Spokespersons

	Blacks	Whites	Gap	Gulf
Brawley probably lying	51%	85%		34
Opinions of (% unfavorable):*				
Al Sharpton	55	84		29
Alton Maddox	31	59		28
Vernon Mason	29	55		26
Brawley incident in long run will make race relations worse, better, or same. (% saying same)	73	54	19	

Source: *New York Times*/CBS News, June 1998.

*Thirty-nine percent of blacks and 14% of whites had no opinion of Sharpton; 53% of blacks and 38% of whites had no opinion of Maddox; and 53% of blacks and 43% of whites had no opinion of Mason.

tion was criticized by a leading student of the city's politics "for polarizing racial attitudes, or at any rate, for capitalizing on prevailing racial cleavages" (Mollenkopf, 1990: 77). However, as table 6.3 shows, differences between blacks and whites on the state of race relations were rather modest, and far smaller than those on the Brawley case. The strongest race difference in opinion concerned whether employment discrimination against blacks had been eliminated or reduced in New York City—79% of whites but only 52% of blacks thought it had. In general, however, the differences are gaps not gulfs. But both blacks and whites were pessimistic about race relations in the city. Only 39% of whites and 26% of blacks described race relations in the city as good and roughly half of both groups agreed that race relations in the city had gotten worse in the past year. In this context, both races agreed that in the long run the Brawley case would have little effect on race relations in New York. In essence, they said race relations were not good in the city and that the Brawley case would do little to alter the situation.

However, the table does reveal a possible explanation for the race gulfs on the Brawley case. The largest gulfs between blacks and whites were on attitudes toward the criminal justice system, specifically the police, the judges and the courts. Blacks are far more likely to doubt the fairness of the police and the courts, a huge gulf of 37 on whether the police treat blacks fairly. This of course resonates with the historical and contemporary material discussed earlier in this chapter concerning blacks and the criminal justice system.

Meanwhile, the Brawley saga continued. She continued to proclaim the truth of her story, became a member of the Nation of Islam, and is now known as

Table 6.3   Racial Differences in Opinion on Race Relations in New York City and on the Criminal Justice System

Race Relations	Blacks	Whites	Gap	Gulf
Are race relations generally good or bad? (% saying good)	26%	39%	13	
Are race relations better or worse than a year ago? (% saying worse)	58	52	—	
Employment discrimination against blacks eliminated in New York. (% agreeing)*	52	79		27
Judges in New York generally treat both blacks and whites fairly. (% agreeing)	39	70		31
Police in New York generally treat blacks and whites fairly or is one group favored? (% saying whites favored)	69	32		37

Source: *New York Times*/WCBS News, June 1988.

*The question read: Since the 1960s, there have been many changes in the law to try to prevent discrimination against blacks and other minorities. Think about how those changes have worked. Do you think discrimination against blacks has been eliminated, has it been reduced, has it stayed about the same, or has it actually increased?

Maryam Muhammad. Steven Pagones, the former Dutchess County prosecutor accused by Brawley, Sharpton, and the attorneys as one of the assailants, won a default judgment against Brawley in 1991 after she failed to answer depositions, continuing her consistent refusal to cooperate with the judicial system. And in June of 1998, after a raucous and rancorous trial, a Dutchess County jury constituted of two blacks and four whites (one of the two blacks voted "not guilty") in a defamation suit filed by Pagones found that Sharpton, Maddox, and Mason in many of their allegations had acted "with reckless disregard for the truth" and thereby defamed Pagones (Hill, 1998). Subsequently, the jury awarded Pagones $345,000 in damages. The three men announced they would appeal.

A "CANYON," NOT A CHASM: THE MARION BARRY CASE

In 1978, Marion Barry, the founding chairman of the Student Nonviolent Coordinating Committee (SNCC), was elected mayor of Washington, D.C., the nation's capital. (SNCC was the most radical and idealistic civil rights group of the 1960s.) In 1965, Barry moved to Washington, became active in community affairs, and in 1978, in the city's second mayoral election, he was elected mayor.[6] Earlier Barry had been elected to the school board and the City Council (see table 6.4, Time Line on the Career of Marion Barry).

In the 1978 mayoral election, Barry defeated two well-regarded black opponents who split the black vote (the city was 70% black), while Barry carried a majority of the white vote. Juan Williams wrote: "Whites infatuated with his dashing image as a civil rights revolutionary intent on making the city government work for the people, gave their vote to Barry, enabling him to win the mayor's seat" (Williams, 1987: 21).

On Sunday, January 21, 1990, Marion Barry was planning to announce his candidacy for reelection to a fourth term. Instead, on Thursday, January 18, the mayor was arrested in a downtown Washington hotel room, where he was videotaped by the FBI soliciting sex from a woman not his wife and smoking or attempting to smoke crack cocaine. After spending several months in jail, four years later, Barry was elected to his fourth term as mayor.

Of all the controversies examined in this book, the arrest, trial, conviction, and subsequent reelection of Marion Barry display the largest cleavage between the races, differences so great as to constitute a canyon—a grand canyon of the racial divide.

The Crimes and the Punishments

Barry's first term was reasonably successful by the standards of big-city mayors, given the constraints of the city's limited authority under the Congress's grant of

Chapter Six

Table 6.4   Time Line on the Career of Marion Barry

The Civil Rights/Community Organizing Phase

April 1960	Marion Barry elected chairman of the Student Nonviolent Coordinating Committee (SNCC).
June 1965	Barry moves to Washington, D.C., to head the local SNCC office.
Jan. 1967	Barry resigns from SNCC.
Summer 1967	Barry cofounds PRIDE, a federally funded antipoverty program directed toward inner-city youth.

The Pre-Mayoral Electoral Politics Phase

1971	Barry wins a seat on the D.C. School Board in a four-way race, capturing 58% of the vote.
1973	Washington, D.C. is granted limited home rule by Congress under the provisions of the District of Columbia Self-Government and Governmental Reorganization Act.
1974	Barry elected to an at-large seat on the D.C. City Council, where he becomes the chair of the powerful Finance and Revenue Committee.
1976	Barry is reelected to an at-large City Council seat.

Mayoral Politics: Phase One (1978–1990)

1978	Barry wins the Democratic mayoral primary contest with 35% of the vote. He defeats a black Republican opponent in the general election, capturing 69% of the vote.
1982	Barry is reelected mayor, winning almost 80% of the vote in the general election against a weak Republican opponent.
1986	Barry reelected to an unprecedented third term, with 61% of the vote.

The Fall from Grace

January 1990	Barry is arrested while attempting to smoke crack cocaine in an FBI sting operation at the Vista Hotel. Event is videotaped and later broadcast on national television.
February 1990	Barry is indicted on three counts of lying to a federal grand jury and five counts of cocaine possession.
May 1990	Barry is indicted on six new charges: five counts of cocaine possession and one count of conspiracy to possess cocaine.
June 1990	Trial begins; jury includes ten blacks and two whites.
August 1990	Jury renders verdict: guilty on one misdemeanor count of cocaine possession; not guilty of possession of crack cocaine; jury deadlocked on the remaining charges. Following the verdict, Barry seeks the necessary petition to run in the 1990 primary election for an at-large City Council seat.
November 1990	Barry loses his bid to capture an at-large City Council seat, winning only 29.4% of the total votes cast. He carries only one of the city's eight wards, Ward 8 (the city's poorest), where he wins 56.5% of the votes; he gets less than 3% of the vote in largely white Ward 3.
October 1991	Barry begins a six-month jail term for the misdemeanor count of cocaine possession.
April 1992	Barry completes his sentence, returns to D.C. in a bus caravan with his supporters, and establishes residency in Ward 8.
September 1992	Barry successfully challenges the incumbent councilperson in Ward 8, winning 69% of the vote, out-polling the incumbent three to one. Voter turnout is about 39%.

Table 6.4 *continued*

November 1992	Barry is unopposed in the general election and therefore wins the Ward 8 council seat.

Mayoral Politics: Phase Two (1994–1998)

Sept. 1994	Barry wins the Democratic mayoral primary with 47% of the vote. Barry gets almost 80% of the vote in Ward 8, but just a little over 3% percent in Ward 3.
May 1998	Barry announces he will not seek reelection.

Source: This time line was prepared by Professor Joseph McCormick of the Department of Political Science, Howard University. We are grateful for permission to use it here in slightly revised form.

home rule (see Persons and Henderson, 1990). However, in his second and third terms, Barry's administrations were marked by scandal after scandal, involving the corruption of many of his top aides and allegations of womanizing and illegal drug use by the mayor.[7] The persistent allegations of illegal drug use by the mayor caused the U.S. Attorney and the FBI to develop an unseemly "sting" operation designed to gather incontrovertible evidence of Barry's guilt. Approved at the highest levels of the U.S. government (including President Bush and the attorney general), the FBI coerced a young woman—a former Barry mistress—into luring him to a downtown hotel for sex and drugs.[8] The mayor was then videotaped by hidden cameras while smoking or attempting to smoke crack cocaine. Arrested and indicted on fourteen charges, Barry was found not guilty of one possession charge and guilty of one misdemeanor possession; the jury of ten blacks and two whites was deadlocked on the remaining ten charges. He was sentenced to six months in prison.

In the first survey conducted by the *Washington Post* several days after the arrest respondents were read the following:

Now I am going to read you two statements people are making about the Barry incident. And I want you to tell me which comes closest to the way you feel. Generally speaking, do you believe that:
  (a) Law enforcement officials were out to get Marion Barry any way they could.
  (b) Barry has only himself to blame.
  (c) Do both statements equally express your thinking about this incident?

Although it would appear that (c) is the more appropriate response—the government was indeed out to get Barry by virtually any means necessary and Barry had only himself to blame for "being gotten"—nevertheless majorities of both blacks and whites selected one of the polar explanations. Table 6.5 displays the responses to the question, including differences by gender, age, and income. A racial gulf is evident. Whereas 65% of whites opined that Barry had only himself to blame, only 36% of blacks agreed. But 22% of blacks placed the blame on the government, compared to 3% of whites. Also, the table shows a tendency for black

Table 6.5   Racial Differences in Opinion on the Arrest of Mayor Barry, by Gender, Income, and Age

	Government Out to Get Barry	Barry to Blame	Both
Blacks	22%	36%	42%
Whites	3	65	32
Men			
Blacks	21	41	39
Whites	7	61	33
Women			
Blacks	22	33	45
Whites	0	68	32
Income under $50,000			
Blacks	23	35	43
Whites	2	67	31
Income $50,000 and over			
Blacks	15	42	43
Whites	3	60	38
Age 18–29			
Blacks	14	38	48
Whites	5	58	37
Age 30–44			
Blacks	18	32	50
Whites	1	65	34
Age 45–60			
Blacks	33	30	36
Whites	3	60	38
Age 60+			
Blacks	29	46	27
Whites	4	84	12

	Blacks	Whites	Gap	Gulf
Barry should resign immediately.	54%	77%		23
Barry should resign, if convicted.	87	94	—	
Barry should run for reelection.	22	5	17	
Would vote for Barry in Democratic primary.	24	3		21
Was Barry using drugs in the hotel room [on the night of arrest]? (% yes)	82	99	17	

Source: *Washington Post*, January 1990.

women to be more sympathetic to Barry, while older whites are overwhelmingly hostile.

When asked in this first survey whether Barry should resign immediately, the gulf narrowed somewhat—77% of whites responded yes, compared to 54% of blacks. However, in this first survey, there was no race difference on whether Barry should resign if found guilty—94% of whites and 87% of blacks agreed that he should. However, 22% of blacks said Barry should run for reelection and 24% indicated they would vote for him. Only 5% of whites agreed that Barry should run and only 3% indicated they would vote for him.

A month later (February 1990), the *Post* conducted its second survey on the incident (see table 6.6), which showed continued support for Barry among many blacks—35% said Barry should run again for mayor and 32% said if he did they would vote for him. By contrast, essentially no white Washingtonians agreed—2% said he should run and 2% said they would vote for him.

By the time of this second survey Barry had been able to rally considerable support in the black community's leadership circles, including Benjamin Hooks, the head of the NAACP, and Minister Louis Farrakhan. In addition, other prominent black leaders refused to denounce Barry for his lies and crimes and instead condemned the FBI for the unseemly nature of the sting operation (Smith, 1990b). Also, by this time, Barry had confessed his long-term addiction to drugs and alcohol, pleaded for forgiveness, and entered a Florida drug rehabilitation program. In this context, the *Post* asked people if they would vote for Barry if he successfully completed the rehabilitation program. Nearly half (46%) of blacks responded yes, but only 2% of whites. On this question, support for Barry cuts across income, gender, and age lines.

Blacks who supported Barry tended to do so while agreeing that he had not

Table 6.6   Racial Differences in Support for Barry in a Postarrest Mayoral Election

	Blacks	Whites	Gap	Gulf	Chasm
Barry should run for reelection. (% saying yes)	35%	2%		33	
Would you vote for Barry in Democratic primary? (% saying yes)	32	2		30	
If Mayor Barry successfully completes his drug and alcohol rehabilitation program, would you support him if he runs for mayor? (% saying yes)	46	2			44
Do you think Barry has been completely truthful about his substance abuse problems? (% saying yes)	15	2	13		
Single most important factor in your decision whether to support Barry or not:					
Drugs/Crime	31	15	16		
Schools	23	4	19		
Barry's Conduct	19	35	16		
City Services	13	14	—		
Government Corruption	14	33	19		

Source: *Washington Post*, February 1990.

been "completely honest and truthful" about his substance abuse problem (only 15% said he had been truthful). Why, then, did they support him? Ironically, when asked what was the "single most important factor" in their decision to support Barry, more blacks mentioned concern about the city's drug and crime problem than any other issue, while Barry's personal conduct and corruption were less important. For whites, these latter concerns were crucial in their decision not to support Barry (see table 6.6).

The final poll we examine dealing with Barry's arrest, trial, and conviction (we examine surveys on Barry's mayoral elections in the next part of this chapter) was conducted by the *Post* in August 1990, shortly after the conclusion of the trial. (Recall that Barry was convicted of only one of the fourteen charges—one misdemeanor count of possession of crack—while the jury deadlocked on the more serious felony counts including perjury.) The results of this poll on attitudes toward the outcome of the trial, reported in table 6.7, reveal a massive race chasm of 58. Three-quarters of blacks expressed satisfaction with the verdict, compared to only 16% of whites. Although there were some modest class–gender–age differences, by and large the races were monoliths in their opinions.

Both blacks (82%) and whites (94%) agreed that Barry had received a fair trial. Why then the canyon in opinion difference on the verdict? Part of the reason may be seen in the fact that in this poll 63% of blacks but a mere 13% of whites agreed that the government's investigation of Barry was "racially motivated," a chasm of 50. Yet the races were less divided on whether Barry should go to jail for his misdemeanor conviction (almost always, a first-time conviction for possession of small amounts of crack does not result in imprisonment); 44% of whites said yes and 28% of blacks, a gap of 16.

Finally, on Barry's political future, the race canyon remained. Almost a third (30%) of blacks indicated in this first posttrial poll they would vote for Barry if he ran again for mayor but essentially no whites (4%) had a similar opinion. Barry's support was strongest among young and poor blacks, although about one-third of

Table 6.7   Racial Differences in Opinion on the Verdict in the Barry Case (% Agreeing)

	Blacks	Whites	Gap	Gulf	Chasm
Personally satisfied with verdict.	74%	16%			58
Jury did a good job.	63	37		26	
Barry received fair trial.	82	94	12		
Investigation of Barry racially motivated.	63	13			50
Barry should resign.	45	74		29	
Barry should serve some jail time.	28	44	16		
Barry should run for mayor.	30	4		26	
Would vote for Barry for City Council.	46	4			42

Source: *Washington Post*, August 1990.

college-educated black respondents also supported a potential Barry mayoral candidacy. At the time of this poll, there was speculation that Barry would seek to begin his political rehabilitation by running first for the city's Council. Almost half (46%) of blacks (4% of whites) indicated they would support such a candidacy. This was good news for Barry as he headed off to jail to contemplate his future in politics in a city deeply divided by race and about him.

The Tragic Political Odyssey of Marion Barry: 1978–1998

Marion Barry was elected mayor of Washington in 1978. Although we attempted to locate survey data going back to his first campaign and mayoral election, we were unable to get access to any polls dealing with Barry before 1988 because neither the *Post* nor its polling firm could locate the pre-1990 raw survey files. Thus, we were not able to conduct our own independent analysis of early poll data on Barry as we were able to do with the surveys conducted after his arrest. However, by going through the *Post*'s cumulative index, we were able to find references to six surveys conducted before 1990. In addition, in May 1994, the *Post* conducted a survey of opinion on Barry and the District of Columbia Control Board (established by Congress in 1995 to oversee the city's budget and most of its administrative operations); and in March 1998, the department of political science at Howard University conducted a similar survey. Thus, in one form or another, we have access to thirteen polls dealing with Barry's tenure as mayor, going back to his first election in 1978. This allows us to track over time his rise, fall, and resurrection.

The Rise and Fall

We begin first with a simple summary of some of the earliest polling data on Barry, beginning with the 1978 campaigns. When Barry won the Democratic primary in September 1978, he faced two rivals: City Council Chairman Sterling Tucker and incumbent Mayor Walter Washington, the City's first elected mayor. In this race, Barry's major base of support was among whites. On June 11, 1978, the *Post* reported, "Barry far outpolls his rivals among white voters. . . . He trails badly among black voters." Later, on September 3, 1978, the *Post* reported that Barry's support among whites had increased from 37% to 50%, following the *Post*'s endorsement of Barry (the *Post*'s endorsement of Barry was both reflective of and a factor in Barry's white support).

Barry continued to have greater support among whites than among blacks when the *Post* surveyed District residents two years after his election, on December 28, 1980. This poll found that 53% of whites and 38% of blacks rated Barry's performance as excellent or good, a gap of 15. Barry still had high marks at the end of 1984; however, his image was beginning to tarnish in the white community. In a January 5, 1985, survey, 42% of whites and 27% of blacks disapproved of Barry's handling of his job. This survey was conducted just before reports that Deputy Mayor Ivanhoe Donaldson was under investigation by a federal grand jury for misuse of city funds during his tenure as head of the District's department of employment services (Donaldson, a former SNCC worker, was seen as perhaps Barry's closest adviser). In the preceding year, Barry's name had been linked with the drug conviction of Karen Johnson, an alleged former Barry mistress.[9] Later the U.S. attorney announced investigations of alleged misuse of funds in several city departments, and a number of District officials were indicted or targeted for investigation.

The 1986 mayoral election was a watershed. On the one hand, most residents continued to rate Barry's delivery of city services as favorable; but in the September 1986 poll, doubts began to surface for the first time about his handling of drugs and crime in the District. In this poll there was evidence of a powerful racial division in opinion of Barry, with 57% of blacks approving and 58% of whites disapproving of his job performance. And in the 1986 Democratic primary, Ward 3 (the city's only predominantly white constituency) voted overwhelming against Barry in favor of a little-known black opponent, Mattie Taylor. However, Barry received heavy support in the rest of the city. Thus, by Barry's third campaign, the pattern of race support had reversed itself. Now Barry was mainly supported by blacks and opposed by whites.

In its October 30, 1986, poll, the *Post* reported that Barry appeared to be popular among blacks because city services were seen as being efficient and to be unpopular among whites because of the perception of corruption and because of the perceived increase in crime and drug problems. The fall campaign of a white Republican candidate exacerbated racial divisions because her major campaign issue was corruption in city government—an issue that appealed to whites. Meanwhile, Barry emphasized jobs and city services—issues that appealed to blacks. By this time, ten top-ranking city officials had been indicted, seemingly confirming a pattern of corruption in Barry's administration. However, many blacks interpreted these indictments as an attack by the "white power structure" (led by President Reagan's U.S. attorney, Joseph DiGenova) in a plot to remove a powerful black government from office. In addition, Barry's campaign openly stressed his support for city services in the District, in contrast to the cuts in social services by President Reagan.

By 1987, an August 30 poll found Barry's approval rating among whites had dropped to 19%, compared to 51% among blacks, a gulf of 32. The *Post* in this survey traced Barry's disapproval among whites to corruption in city government and increasing allegations of wrongdoing by Barry himself, involving drugs and adultery. On the other hand, Barry and his supporters argued that many of these allegations were the creation of a hostile white establishment, especially the *Washington Post* and the U.S. attorney.

The Resurrection

Four years after his fall in 1990, Barry was resurrected and elected to an unprecedented fourth term as mayor.[10] Even before he was jailed, Barry changed his party affiliation from Democrat to Independent and challenged incumbent Hilda Mason in 1990 for one of the city's two at-large council seats. Although the early polls indicated Barry might defeat the elderly and frail Mason, he lost—his first defeat ever in city politics. However, Barry did carry Ward 8, the city's poorest and most segregated constituency. Two years later, Barry challenged Wilhelmina Rolark, another elderly woman, who represented Ward 8 on the City Council, and he was elected by a three-to-one margin in spite of the opposition of the city's entire political establishment, black and white.

Meanwhile, in 1990, Sharon Pratt Dixon, a prominent Washington attorney, a corporate executive, and a former Democratic Party functionary, was elected mayor. In a multicandidate field, Dixon won the primary with 37% of the vote largely on the basis of the overwhelming support of the city's white establishment and voters (Dixon was enthusiastically endorsed by the *Washington Post* in a series of editorials). Although Dixon was popular among the editorial page writers of the *Post*, members of Congress, and the city's white business elite, as well as white voters, fairly soon her administration lost support among blacks; and in her campaign for reelection four years later, she was defeated by Barry in a three-way race. Why? Why did the black voters return Barry to office?

The answers are many and complex. Even after his fall, Barry continued to be the dominant figure in city politics. By the end of her term, Dixon was viewed unfavorably by many blacks in the city; and the other challenger to Dixon—City Council member John Ray—was viewed as competent perhaps but without charisma. Finally, having served as mayor for twelve years, Barry had a loyal political following, as well as a well-oiled, time-tested political organization.

A December 1993 *Post* poll found that 72% of blacks had a favorable impression of Barry, compared to 10% of whites (a huge chasm of 62). This same poll found that almost half of blacks (but only 15% of whites) thought Mayor Dixon was more concerned with serving the interests of the middle- and upper-income groups than those of the poor. In his campaign against Dixon, Barry emphasized concern for the poor, to contrast Dixon's perceived lack of concern. Barry also waged a neonationalist campaign, donning African garb and appealing to race solidarity. He urged the city's black voters to elect him as a means to repudiate the city's white establishment, which had, in his view, unfairly driven him from office.

Barry won the 1994 Democratic primary with 47% of the vote in a three-way race. In the fall general election, he faced a white, female Republican member of the City Council, Carol Schwarz. A September 1994 *Post* poll found 90% of blacks supporting Barry, compared to 16% of whites—a "grand canyon" of 74. Barry easily defeated Schwarz in the November election.

For most of his tenure in office, the racial divisions that marked his election persisted. For example, a May 1996 poll found that 76% of blacks had a favorable impression of Barry, compared to just 14% of whites (a chasm of 62), and that 70% of blacks said he was doing a good job, compared to just 11% of whites (a chasm of 59).

Shortly after Barry's reelection, the city's long-standing budget and administrative problems reached crisis proportions. As a result, the Congress in 1995 stripped the city of its budget authority and most of its administrative powers and placed them in the hands of a Financial Control Board, appointed by the president. Effectively, Barry's election became as one writer called it, a "hollow victory" (see Barras, 1998) because he lacked the effective capacity to govern. Meanwhile the city's fiscal, physical (symbolized by the random vandalism and destruction of its parking meters), and educational infrastructures were in paralyzed decline.

This sad state of affairs also continued to divide the city racially. A May 1997 *Post* poll found that 65% of whites approved of the control board but 47% of blacks disapproved of it; 57% of whites thought the board had made things better, but only 37% of blacks agreed. And in this poll Marion Barry continued to polarize the races. Ninety percent of whites disapproved of his performance, and 93% said he should not seek reelection; but 43% of blacks gave the mayor a favorable job rating, and one-third said he should run for reelection.

A year later, a Howard University poll (directed by Seltzer) found similar results: 51% of blacks approved of Barry's job performance but only 10% of whites; 74% of whites approved of the control board but only 44% of blacks; and 60% of blacks thought Barry should be given more control in running the city but only 10% of whites.

Finally, many blacks in Washington have long held that there is a secret "plan" by the white establishment to remove local government from black control. To tap sentiments on this long-held conspiracy theory among black Washingtonians, the Howard University survey asked respondents whether they thought, in the context of the control board, that such a plan existed: 72% of blacks said definitely or probably, compared to 12% of whites—a chasm of 60.

Reflections on the Odyssey of Marion Barry

In May 1998, Marion Barry announced he would not seek reelection, bringing his 27-year political sojourn to an end. Of all the stories told in this book, we believe

Marion Barry's is the saddest. Starting as an idealistic SNCC civil rights leader, he had a remarkable career—community activist in Washington's poorest neighborhoods, school board leader, city council member, and then mayor (arguably a good and effective mayor in the early years). Then in 1990 we saw his dramatic fall in a shameless betrayal of his potential—a shameless betrayal because he was a man who held himself out as a role model, lecturing poor Washingtonians on the evils of drug use and irresponsible sexual behavior. (At one point in 1989, Barry had gone so far as to call for the dispatch of the U.S. Army to root out drug trafficking.)

But Barry's behavior was more than a personal betrayal, a personal failing. It was also a betrayal of the dreams and aspirations of black America. As Jaffe and Sherwood (1994) told the story in their book, *Dream City: Race, Power, and the Decline of Washington, D.C.*, it is a tragedy worthy of the Greeks. Washington, D.C., the nation's capital, was to be a dream city, a city where the principles of the civil rights movement could be brought to bear in a truly model city, a laboratory for political and policy experiments in social democracy. Barry turned the dream into a nightmare.

Why then was he reelected after his crimes? Why did the city's African American majority return a convicted drug user to its highest office? We offer the following propositions as tentative explanations.

First, Barry's support after his first several years in office was very strong among middle-class as well as poor blacks (although less so among the city's old-line, color-conscious black establishment who viewed Barry as a "Bama"—a person without taste or refinement). This is in part because he created many jobs for middle-class blacks and provided contracts and business opportunities for others. He also attempted to provide a broad social safety net for the city's poor. By contrast, whites were enthusiastic about Barry during his first campaign but became disenchanted as many viewed his administration as neglecting priorities they preferred—street maintenance, police and ambulance services—in favor of patronage-based programs for blacks.

Although most blacks were probably disgusted with Barry's misbehavior, many also saw his arrest as a "setup," a conspiracy by powerful white men to bring down a powerful and effective black leader.[11] Barry was able to use this to his advantage in his resurrection. Also, Barry's postarrest rhetoric about the frailties of men and his talk of forgiveness and redemption resonate well in the religious ethos of black community culture. Finally, in his neonationalism, he offered himself as a "strong" black man who could not be broken by the white power structure, which resonates well with the nationalist sentiments of solidarity in African American culture. In black cultural ethos, Barry may have symbolized "defiant heroism" or the "bad nigger."

Whatever the explanations, this was a sad story of a man who divided his city by color and who betrayed the dream.

THE RODNEY KING CASE AND THE L.A. RIOTS

The Rodney King case may be as well known as the Simpson case. Virtually everybody that watches television saw the videotaped beating of King by Los Angeles police officers and then followed on television the several days of rioting that followed the not guilty verdicts.[12]

Rodney Glenn King, an unemployed black construction worker, at 12:05 A.M. on March 3, 1991, failed to yield to Los Angeles police (because he later said that he feared a traffic violation might result in revocation of his parole) and was chased by several units of the Los Angeles police and the California Highway Patrol (see table 6.8 for time line). King's car was finally stopped, and several white officers began to "beat him half to death," in the words of one of the police (Wood and Stolberg, 1991). Of the twenty officers at the scene, at least three beat King, hitting him between fifty-three and fifty-six times while he lay defenseless on the ground. At least one officer stomped on his head; the right socket in one of King's eyes was broken and bones were broken in the base of his skull (Wood and Stolberg, 1991). All of this occurred in full view of residents of the nearby apartment complex from which George Holliday videotaped the incident. Many of those residents shouted, "Stop, don't kill him." After the beating and King's arrest, the officers bragged, boasted, laughed, joked, and made racist slurs about King and the beating; all of this was picked up on police radio transmissions (Mydans, 1991). As a result of the beating, King was left permanently disabled and psychologically damaged for life.

Four of the twenty officers (Timothy Wind, Laurence Powell, Stacey Koon, and Theodore Briseno) were charged with assault and the use of unreasonable force. Tried by a jury of ten whites, one Asian, and one Hispanic, three of the

Table 6.8   Time Line on the Rodney King Case and the L.A. Riots

March 3, 1991	Rodney King beaten by several Los Angeles police officers
March 4	George Holiday's videotape of beating broadcast on local station KTLA and subsequently on CNN
March 15	Grand jury indicts four officers for unlawful assault and use of excessive force in King beating
July 23	State Court of Appeals approves defense motion to move trial to Simi Valley, a largely white suburb of L.A.
February 15, 1992	Simi Valley trial begins with jury of ten whites, one Filipino, and one Latino
April 29 (3:10 P.M.)	After six hours of deliberation, jury finds three officers not guilty of all charges and one guilty of one count of excessive force
April 29 (4:00 P.M.)	Rioting begins in South Central L.A.
May 3	National Guard suppresses riots (52 dead, 2,500 injured, $1 billion in property damage)

policemen were acquitted altogether and one was found guilty of one count of excessive force.[13] On the afternoon of the verdict, Los Angeles erupted into several days of riotous rebellion.

Three national surveys were conducted on the beating, the trial, and the verdict in the case of the accused officers and the subsequent riots.

Shortly after the verdict in April 1992 ABC News and the *Washington Post* conducted the first of these surveys. The survey attempted to frame opinion on the King verdict in the context of a series of questions on race relations in general and opinions in general on the criminal justice system in the United States. These general questions reveal a vast chasm between the races (see table 6.9). For example, 54% of whites thought the police treated blacks and whites equally, a view held by only 12% of blacks; and 52% of whites thought minorities received equal treatment in the criminal justice system, a view held by 9% of blacks. And with regard to race relations in general in the United States, there was a gulf in opinion—60% of blacks rated the situation fair or poor, compared to 29% of whites. Forty-three percent of blacks agreed there was a "great deal" of prejudice among whites toward blacks, an opinion shared by only 10% of whites.

In the context of these general queries about race and justice in America, respondents were asked their opinions on the King incident. Ninety percent of respondents reported having seen the video and there were no differences in opin-

Table 6.9   Racial Differences in Opinion on Race Relations, the Criminal Justice System, and the King Verdict

	Blacks	Whites	Gulf	Chasm
Do you think race relations in the United States are excellent, good, not so good, or poor?(% poor)	60%	29%	31	
Police in most cities treat blacks as fairly as whites. (% agree)	12	54		42
Blacks and other minorities receive equal treatment as whites in criminal justice system. (% agree)	9	52		43
Were police officers guilty? (% yes)	99	93	—	
Verdict shows blacks cannot get justice in this country. (% agree)	81	27		54
Do you think the videotape of the beating was enough for you to make a judgment about whether the policemen were guilty, or do you think the videotape might have left out important parts of what happened that could change your judgment? (% videotape enough*)	92	54	38	

Sources: All except the last question (about the videotape) are from the *Washington Post*/ABC News poll, April 1992. The item on the videotape is from the *New York Times*/CBS News poll of May 1992.

*Ninety-five percent of blacks and 92% of whites reported having seen the video.

ion between blacks and whites on the verdict—93% of whites and 99% of blacks disagreed with it. This result was also found in a second *Washington Post* poll conducted in May 1992 and in a *New York Times* poll also conducted in May 1992. Apparently, given the opinion of most whites toward the way the police treat blacks, the videotaped beating was seen as an aberration and/or as not being racially motivated. For most blacks, however, it was probably simply incontrovertible evidence for what they knew all along. This racial difference may be seen in attitudes toward the videotape as evidence—92% of blacks said the video itself was enough evidence for conviction, compared to 54% of whites (see table 6.9). This gulf of 38 in opinion on the evidentiary value of the video is probably emblematic of the structural differences in opinion toward the criminal justice system and its relationship to blacks. Further, reflections of the structural bases of this black-white difference is the chasm of 54 on whether the verdict shows blacks cannot get justice in the United States—81% of blacks agreeing but only 27% of whites.

Although there was a consensus among the races about the verdict, the familiar gaps and gulfs emerged when the focus shifted to opinion on the riots that followed. Table 6.10 displays the results of some questions about the riots. Although blacks are somewhat more likely to embrace "nonviolent protests" as a means to advance their interests rather than simply "laws and persuasions," both blacks and whites (95% and 98%) reject the use of "violence." However, 82% of blacks and 44% of whites agreed that only violent demonstrations or riots get the

Table 6.10   Racial Differences in Opinion on the L.A. Riots

	Blacks	*Whites*	*Gap*	*Gulf*
What is the best way for blacks to gain their rights—				
Laws?	45%	28%	17	
Protests?	53	67	14	
Violence?	5	2	—	
The only time the federal government really pays attention to black problems is when blacks resort to violent demonstrations or riots. (% agree)	82	44		38
There have been lots of accusations about who or what is to blame for the riots in Los Angeles that followed the verdict in the Rodney King case. Would you place a lot of blame on (% saying a lot):				
Reagan/Bush policies?	69	39		30
1960s social programs?	31	25	—	
The jury?	77	47		30
Poverty and discrimination?	77	74	—	
Irresponsible people?	72	84	12	

Source: The second question is from the *Washington Post*/ABC News April 1992 poll. All other questions from the *New York Times*/CBS News May 1992 poll.

attention of the federal government. Although 38 is a large gulf, it is interesting that there is a consensus among blacks and a large plurality among whites that a method they reject—violence—is the only effective way to get the government's attention, a view supported by the most detailed study of the impact of the 1960s riots (see Button, 1978). Also, the riots after the verdict did draw the attention of the candidates then seeking the presidency, with both Bush and Clinton raising for the first time questions about the need for new programs to address problems of race, poverty, and urban dislocations.[14] However, as the riots subsided in memory, attention of the presidential candidates returned to the routines of neglecting problems of race and poverty (Cline, 1993).

A major study of television coverage of the L.A. riots found that the riots were the nation's first "multicultural riot," involving Latinos, blacks, whites, and Asians. However, the coverage on both local and national television portrayed the riot stereotypically as a black riot (see Smith, 1994). For example, although Latinos comprised a *majority* of the people arrested, they constituted only 24% of the rioters on the national networks and 33% on the local stations. Almost 60% of the rioters portrayed on the local Los Angeles television news were black.

This study also showed that television portrayed criminality and lawlessness as the causes of the riots, rather than the underlying problems of racism and poverty or the acquittal of the officers who beat Rodney King. Eighty percent of the local coverage focused on criminality as the primary cause of the riot. And although the three networks were more likely to focus on other causes, 60% of their coverage also focused on lawlessness as the principal explanation (Smith, 1994).

Table 6.10 shows that although both blacks and whites placed a "lot" of the responsibility for the riots on lawlessness—"irresponsible people taking advantage" of the situation, the predominant image propagated in the media—the data in the table also show a consensus between the races that frustrations due to poverty and discrimination were factors. Blacks were more likely than whites to place a "lot" of blame on the social policies of the Reagan and Bush administrations (69% to 39%) and the decision of the King jury (77% to 47%); but it is interesting that both blacks and whites rejected the explanation offered at the time by then Vice President Dan Quayle, that the social programs of the 1960s were to blame. Rather, both blacks and whites agreed that a lot of the blame was due to poverty and discrimination. Finally—and most ominously—both races (83% and 79%) agreed with the statement that the riots were a warning to the country that more riots would happen if race relations did not improve (see table 6.11).

How might race relations be improved? Here one observes a remarkable absence of gaps, gulfs, and chasms—a race consensus. Respondents of both races agreed that adding more police would not help a great deal to avoid racial violence. Rather, as table 6.11 shows, there was a consensus that more jobs and training were more likely to improve race relations. Further, when respondents were asked, "Which would be the better way to spend money in the future to prevent riots?"

Table 6.11 Racial Differences in Opinion on Ways to Improve Race Relations and to Prevent Future Riots

	Blacks	Whites	Gap	Gulf
Here are some things people say could help reduce racial tension and prevent riots. Do you think [___] would help a lot, a little, or wouldn't make that much difference? (% saying a lot)				
More police	24%	25%	—	
Jobs/job training	87	78	—	
Better police training	60	58	—	
Stronger civil rights laws	68	42		26
More minorities in government	68	51	17	
More minority businesses	62	45	17	
If you had to choose, which would be the better way to spend money in the future to prevent riots—investing in stronger police forces or in jobs and job training? (% choosing jobs and training)	97	94	—	
Was the L.A. riot a warning to improve race relations to prevent more violence or an isolated incident? (% saying warning)	83	79	—	
% thinking there always will be a lot of prejudice/ discrimination	60	50	10	
% thinking race riots will be happening 25 years from now	65	65	—	

Source: *New York Times*/CBS News, May 1992.

only 6% of whites and 3% of blacks chose "investing in stronger police forces" instead of "investing in jobs and job training programs."

But, many in both groups were pessimistic about the future: 60% of blacks and 50% of whites believed "there will always be a lot of racial prejudice and discrimination in America," and 65% of both races think "racial riots will still be happening 25 years from now."

THE O. J. SIMPSON CASE

O. J. Simpson's case also divided the races, and Simpson also made appeals to the Christian and black nationalist ethos of African American culture although, unlike Marion Barry, Simpson had never before in his career identified with black people's struggles for freedom and justice. He married white (abandoning his black wife at the crest of his first success) and lived "white" (Hirschberg, 1994). In 1969, Simpson told Robert Lipsyte of the *New York Times*:

My biggest accomplishment is that people look at me like a man first, not a black man . . . it's what I strive for—to be a man first. Maybe it's money, a class thing. The Negro is always identified with poverty. But then you think of Willie Mays as black but not Bill Cosby. So, it's more than just money. As black men, we need something up there all the time for us, but what I am doing is not for principles or black people. NO, I'm dealing first for O. J. Simpson, his wife and his baby. (Quoted in Clay, 1997).

The Simpson case is the best known of the controversies examined in this book. Indeed, trying to put the Simpson race chasm in perspective was the inspiration for this book. It is the most familiar of the cases; as we discuss later, most Americans indicated they followed the extensive media coverage of his arrest and trial. The trial was the most thoroughly covered in American history—indeed, one of the most thoroughly covered events since the Watergate crisis that led to the resignation of a president. The Simpson case also generated more books and articles than the other controversies,[15] although relatively few of these works employed systematic survey data on reactions to the case. This survey data is our contribution to the Simpson literature.

On June 12, 1994, Nicole Brown Simpson, the estranged wife of Orenthal James (O. J.) Simpson, was found brutally knifed to death outside her Los Angeles town house (see table 6.12, the Simpson Case Time Line). Also murdered was a young man named Ronald Goldman. A month later, Simpson, the acclaimed former football player, well-known television pitchman for Avis Rental Car, and commentator on NBC's weekly telecast of the National Football League, was charged with the murders.

The first *New York Times*/CBS News survey on the Simpson case was conducted in June 1994, shortly after Simpson was charged with the murders. As we indicated, the Simpson case received near-saturation coverage in the media, especially on television (the preliminary hearing that led to Simpson's indictment was televised live on the three broadcast networks, as well as on several cable channels). Most Americans indicated that they followed the case to some extent, with only 24% of whites and 20% of blacks saying they did not follow the case at all.

But there are some interesting race, gender, and class differences in attention to the case. First, college-educated blacks were much more likely (63%) to say they followed the case "closely," compared to 26% of college-educated whites; 25% of white and 22% of black high school graduates said they followed the case closely. Second, black women were much more likely than black men, white men, or white women to follow the case closely. This black gender difference in attention is a first indicator of the distinctive opinion profile that would emerge among black women on the case.

In spite of the chasm to come, this first poll on the case showed no differences between blacks and whites on whether Simpson could get a fair trial—50% of

Table 6.12   Time Line on the O. J. Simpson Case

June 12, 1994	Bodies of Nicole Brown Simpson and Ronald Goldman found outside her Brentwood townhouse.
June 13	Simpson returns from Chicago; handcuffed, questioned, and released.
June 17	Simpson charged with murders, fails to surrender; warrant issued for his arrest.
June 17	Simpson engages in nationally televised, car chase on a Los Angeles freeway. Car chase ends at Simpson's home, where he is arrested.
June 30	Preliminary hearing begins; televised on all three commercial networks.
July 7	Judge finds sufficient evidence to bound Simpson over for trial.
September 26	Trial begins, Johnnie Cochran, an African American, replaces Robert Shapiro as lead defense attorney. Lead attorneys for prosecution are a white woman and a black man.
March 13, 1995	Detective Mark Fuhrman (who found a bloody glove and other evidence incriminating Simpson) denies he ever used the word *nigger* or made other racial slurs.
April 24	Jurors dress in black and refuse to continue trial until judge meets with them to discuss racial problems.
June 15	Simpson struggles to put on bloody glove; it does not appear to fit.
July 3	Prosecution rests after nearly six months.
August 28	Mark Fuhrman tapes played in court, showing he had lied about using the word *nigger* (jury not present).
September 4	Excerpts from Fuhrman tapes read to jury.
September 6	Fuhrman invokes Fifth Amendment when asked if he lied about ever falsifying police reports, planting evidence, or using racial slurs (jury not present).
September 26	Closing arguments begin.
October 2	Jury begins deliberations.
October 3	Jury returns "not guilty" verdict after four hours of deliberation.

whites and 52% of blacks said a fair trial was possible. College-educated blacks and black women were somewhat more likely to believe this, whereas young whites were somewhat more skeptical.

In its second survey (July 1994), the *Times* still found no differences between the races on the "possibility" of a fair trial, however, belief in the possibility had slipped from about 50% to 40%. When respondents were asked whether the criminal justice system was biased—in favor of or against Simpson—the first gulf in opinion on the case appeared—54% of blacks saw a bias against Simpson, compared to 28% of whites.

The third *Times* poll was conducted a month later (July 1994) just after the decision by the judge in the preliminary hearing to bound Simpson over for trial. Virtually the entire country had watched at least part of the hearing on television (only 5% of whites and 2% of blacks said they had not watched at all). There was still a consensus on the possibility of a fair trial, but there were two gulfs in opinion between the races. First, although 89% of whites agreed with the judge's decision in the preliminary hearing that there was "sufficient evidence" to try

Simpson for the murders, only 66% of blacks agreed—a gulf of 23. Second, most Americans at this point did not have an opinion on Simpson's guilt or innocence; however, of those with opinions, there was also a race gulf of 23—12% of whites said innocent, compared to 35% of blacks. Women and younger blacks were more likely to believe in Simpson's innocence. Finally, this poll asked if prior to the murders Simpson was seen as a "role model." He was for 63% of blacks and 45% of whites.[16]

On October 1, 1995, CBS News conducted a poll on the case. This was near the trial's end, after Officer Mark Fuhrman had testified that he had lied about using the word *nigger* to refer to blacks and after Simpson's attorneys, led by Johnnie Cochran, an African American, had strongly suggested that Simpson had been framed, that there had been a conspiracy by the Los Angeles police to plant blood and other evidence so as to make Simpson appear guilty.[17] As the trial approached its end, the races were clearly polarized (at this point 64% of blacks and 59% of whites said they had followed the trial closely). Whereas in June both blacks and whites thought a fair trial was possible, by this stage 85% of whites agreed on the possibility of a fair trial but only 54% of blacks—a gulf of 31 (see table 6.13). A chasm of 52 existed on perceptions of guilt or innocence. In the first July *Times* poll, most people did not have an opinion on this question, and of those who did there was only a race gulf of 23. As the trial neared its end, 65% of whites said guilty, compared to only 13% of blacks (among blacks, men and the college educated were more likely to believe Simpson guilty).

There was a chasm on whether the police planted the blood and other evidence, as implied by Simpson's attorneys. Among blacks, 88% agreed, compared to 37%

Table 6.13   Racial Differences in Opinion on the Simpson Case as Trial Neared End, October 1995

	Blacks	Whites	Gulf	Chasm
Simpson received fair trial.	54%	85%	31	
Simpson probably guilty.	13	65		52
How likely do you think it is that there was a conspiracy by the Los Angeles police to plant blood and evidence to make Simpson look guilty? (% saying likely)	88	37		51
How often do you think the police and prosecutors in your community break the law or lie to obtain convictions? (% saying very often/sometimes)	83	47	36	
If police lie or tamper with some evidence in a criminal case, do you think it is a good idea or a bad idea for juries to punish the police by acquitting the defendant? (% saying good idea)	60	29	31	

Source: *New York Times*/CBS News, October 1, 1995.

of whites. Eighty-three percent of blacks compared to 47% of whites agreed that police and prosecutors sometimes break the law in order to obtain convictions. Finally in this poll, 60% of blacks agreed that if the police lie or tamper with evidence, juries should acquit defendants, but only 29% of whites.

On October 3, after only four hours of deliberations, the jury found Simpson not guilty. Three days later, the *Washington Post* conducted a survey on reactions to the verdict. The results are reported in table 6.14. On the general notion of whether there is equality in the American criminal justice system, there was a huge chasm—54% of whites agreeing, compared to 9% of blacks. And on the verdict itself, there was another large chasm—91% of blacks but 39% of whites agreed with the verdict. The chasm on the police conspiracy theory remains. However, there are interesting differences among blacks in terms of gender and education. Eighty-one percent of black high school graduates believed the police planted evidence, compared to 64% of college-educated blacks; and 82% of black women compared to 68% of black men accepted the police conspiracy theory (these data are not displayed in the table). And in a perhaps historic reversal of the black-white opinion pattern on the American criminal justice system, 59% of whites said the verdict made them less confident about the system, compared to 29% of blacks.

The *Post* survey included a series of hypothetical "what if" questions about

Table 6.14   Racial Differences in Opinion on the Verdict in the Simpson Criminal Trial

	Blacks	Whites	Gap	Gulf	Chasm
Do you think blacks and other minorities receive same treatment as whites in the criminal justice system? (% no)	54%	9%			45
Do you agree or disagree with Simpson verdict? (% agree)	91	39			52
Whether you agree with verdict, do you think Simpson was guilty? (% yes)	24	78			54
Do you think there was a police conspiracy to frame Simpson? (% yes)	78	28			50
Does the verdict make you feel more or less confident about the criminal justice system? (% more confident)	71	41		30	
Do you think there would have been a guilty verdict if:					
Simpson was white?	8	48			40
Jury was all white?	59	73	14		
Simpson was not rich?	70	82	12		
Victims were black?	25	33	—		

Source: *Washington Post*, October 4–6, 1995.

the verdict. Blacks thought the verdict would have been the same if Simpson was white; whites did not. Both blacks and whites thought Simpson's wealth was important in the outcome, as was the race of the jurors (the jury was composed of ten blacks, one Hispanic, and one white).

The jury's decision was controversial on its merits. But it was also controversial because the jury was nearly all black and largely female and because of the speed of its decision—four hours—which suggested to some a lack of deliberation. (Cooley, Bess, and Rubin-Jackson [1995] in their book recounting their experiences as jurors, suggested that after months of hearing the evidence, reasonable doubt as to Simpson's guilt was never in doubt.) Some people went so far as to suggest that the jurors were too ignorant to make a competent decision, that they acted on emotions rather than on evidence.

The race differences displayed in table 6.15 are not large on the jury, except 49% of whites but only 15% of blacks thought the jury acted on emotions rather than the facts, and whites were more likely to agree that the Simpson case was just another case of men getting away with the abuse of women (evidence presented at trial showed Simpson had engaged in abusive behavior toward his wife during their relationship).

Finally, reactions to two statements perhaps show the ultimate difference in perceptual worlds of blacks and whites on this case, but also on the Barry case and conspiracism as well. Respondents were asked to agree or to disagree with two statements: (1) "White establishment always tries to bring down successful blacks" and (2) "Blacks often use race to excuse wrong doing." The results were that 56% of blacks and 12% of whites agreed with the first statement and that 63% of whites and 33% of blacks agreed with the second statement.

After Simpson's acquittal of the criminal charges of murdering Nicole Simpson and Goldman, the families of the two victims filed a civil suit against Simpson for the "wrongful deaths" of their relatives. This time, a largely white jury in Santa

Table 6.15 Racial Differences in Opinion on the Jury and the Verdict in the Simpson Criminal Trial (% Agreeing)

	Blacks	Whites	Gap	Gulf	Chasm
Jury not smart enough to understand evidence.	14%	27%	13		
Jury ignored evidence; decided on emotions.	15	49		34	
Simpson just another case of men getting away with abuse of women.	34	60		26	
White establishment always tries to bring down successful blacks.	56	12			44
Blacks often use race to excuse wrong doing.	33	63		30	

Source: *Washington Post*, October 4-6, 1995.

Monica found Simpson guilty and ordered him to pay $33 million in damages.

In the first three questions in table 6.16, we report race differences in reactions to the civil verdict, based on a poll conducted by *Newsweek*. Again, chasms, not gaps and gulfs, are observed. Whites (82%) agreed with the verdict but only 29% of blacks. Although 58% of whites said a civil trial after a not guilty verdict in a criminal trial was fair, only 16% of blacks agreed. A chasm of 40 exists on whether Simpson should be granted custody of his two small children (fathered with his deceased wife), rather than the Brown family—89% of blacks favored custody for Simpson, 49% of whites.[18]

Finally, both blacks and whites agreed that Simpson's career as a pitchman and television commentator was finished. There is, however, a large gulf on whether this should be the case—74% of blacks but only 36% of whites said they would buy a product endorsed by Simpson.

The O. J. Simpson case was a simple murder case. Yet it also came to symbolize the nation's historic black and white worldviews about justice in America. Only in this sense is the case important.

Reflecting on both the Rodney King and O. J. Simpson cases, Jewelle Taylor Gibbs wrote:

> [T]his society had to confront the reality that we inhabited one country geographically but were divided into two nations racially, culturally, economically and politically. There was no consensus and no common ground. . . .
>
> The jurors in Simi Valley were *inclined to believe* the police officers' defense because it was consistent with their prior experiences and beliefs about the police. In contrast, the jurors in the Simpson case were *inclined to disbelieve* the testimony

Table 6.16   Racial Differences in Reaction to the Verdict in the Simpson Civil Trial

	Blacks	Whites	Gap	Gulf	Chasm
Do you agree or disagree with guilty verdict? (% agreeing)	29%	82%			53
Your feelings about the Simpson case aside, do you think it is fair or unfair for a defendant found not guilty of criminal charges to be found liable in a civil trial? (% fair)	16	58			42
Should Simpson be able to keep custody of children? (% yes)	89	49			40
Will Simpson ever win enough public acceptance to resume role as public figure? (% yes)	34	23	11		
Would you buy a product or service endorsed by Simpson? (% yes)	74	36		38	

Source: *Newsweek*, February 5–7, 1997.

of the police because of their prior experiences and beliefs about police misconduct. In both cases, these jurors viewed the evidence, processed it, and evaluated it in terms of their own worldview and personal experiences. (1996: 217, emphasis in original)

CONCLUSION

The O. J. Simpson case involved the combustible mix of race, sex, and murder. Historically, a black man could be killed for even glancing at a white woman (recall the brutal murder of young Emmett Till in Mississippi in 1955 for merely saying "Hi, baby" to a white woman). And the murder of a white woman by a black man historically would lead to swift justice—frequently a tortured lynching. And interracial sex and marriage has long been taboo among blacks, especially among black women. Yet despite this combustible historical mix, the Simpson case did not initially divide the races. Rather, it was only after the televised trial with its trails of blood and seeds of doubt about a possible police conspiracy that modest gaps turned into chasms and canyons when—to be noted a largely black female—jury freed Simpson, regardless of what the prosecutors called a "mountain of evidence."

However, if one looks at the history of blacks in relationship to the criminal justice system—a shamefully racist history—and at the widespread evidence of continuing racism in the justice system, then black opinion on the Simpson case (but also on the Brawley and Barry cases) is not surprising. And if one knows that many blacks believe—plausibly or not—that the government is engaged in various conspiracies to subordinate and dominate blacks (including attempts to destroy black leaders, especially black males of status or stature), the response by blacks to Barry's efforts to return to office is explicable.

Finally, if one accepts the credibility of the videotaped beating of Rodney King, the riots were a predictable (and indeed predicted) response. As the students, black and white, in one of our classes learned of the verdict, their constant refrain was, "Is L.A. burning?" And the opinions of the respondents in the King case, both black and white, suggest that this query will be asked about L.A. and other cities in America in the twenty-first century.

NOTES

1. For example, except for the videotape, the beating of Rodney King has an exact parallel in the 1979 beating of Arthur McDuffie in Miami. McDuffie, a black man who apparently violated traffic laws while riding his motorcycle, was pursued by as many as a dozen police officers who brutally beat him to death. Several of the officers were indicted, but as in the Rodney King case the trial was moved (to Tampa) and heard by an all-white

jury. After less than three hours, each of the policemen was found not guilty. Within hours of the verdict, Miami's black community erupted in several days of riotous rebellion, the worst since the 1960s and the worst prior to the L.A. riots after the Rodney King verdict (on the McDuffie case and the Miami rebellion, see Harris, 1999). Since the McDuffie case, there have been several other black rebellions in Miami, all precipitated by forms of police violence against blacks.

2. Assistant Attorney General for Civil Rights Bill Lann Lee explained the Justice Department's inaction on these cases by saying that in many of them the evidence indicated no violations of federal law or that insufficient evidence to meet the law's high burden of proof or because local police or prosecutors had already taken action against the officers. (See Associated Press, 1999b.)

3. Under Congressman Conyers's leadership, the House easily passed legislation directing the Justice Department to collect statistics on the racial and ethnic breakdown of traffic stops. As a result of the opposition of the National Association of Police Organizations, the bill was killed in the Senate's Judiciary Committee (see Jackson, 1998). Although as Arkansas governor President Clinton strongly supported racial profiling by the state police, in 1999 he endorsed the Conyers bill and instructed federal law enforcement agencies (the Drug Enforcement Administration, the National Park Police, and the Customs Service) to collect data on the people they stop or arrest. Data collection aside, racial profiling is likely to continue because most police agencies view it as a justifiable law enforcement tool, given the disproportionately high incidence of black involvement in criminal activities (see Goldberg, 1999).

4. 481 U.S. 279 (1987).

5. The survey covered respondents in New York City and Dutchess County, where the alleged incident occurred. We, however, analyze only the 676 respondents in New York City.

6. Washington, D.C., was granted "home rule" and the right to elect its mayor and city council by the Congress in 1974. On the tension-filled relationship between the city and Congress both before and after home rule, see Harris (1995).

7. On the slow but steady decline of Barry's administrations into scandal and corruption, see Jaffe and Sherwood (1994).

8. Rasheeda Moore, the young woman, was coerced into participating in the sting by the threat of prosecution and the loss of her young children.

9. Of Karen Johnson, Juan Williams (1987: 21) wrote:

[A] woman with whom Barry had a "personal relationship" went to jail for dealing cocaine and refusing to tell a grand jury if she sold any to Barry. Since then the same woman, Karen Johnson, when she was called before a grand jury probing kickbacks and bribery, is reported to have admitted that contractors with ties to Barry paid her $25,000 to keep her mouth shut. Having been jailed once for refusing to answer, she reportedly told this grand jury that she sold cocaine to Barry 20 to 30 times.

10. For the story of Barry's remarkable resurrection, see the account by Barras (1998), a Washington journalist who covered Barry's career for several local papers.

11. In many ways the black community's reactions to Barry's misdeeds parallel the responses of the American public to allegations of lying and womanizing leveled against President Clinton in the so-called Monica Lewinsky affair (where the president had a sexual relationship with a young White House intern and then encouraged her and others to lie and cover up). Throughout the year-long investigation leading up to the president's impeachment, polls showed support for the president, with most Americans appearing to view the president's sexual behavior as personal and private, without relevance to his conduct of his official duties. The polls also showed that a significant number of Americans agreed with the allegation of the president's wife that the investigation of Clinton's sex life was part of a right-wing conspiracy to bring down a popular, progressive president. Most polls also showed a race gulf of about 24 in support for the president, with more than 90% of blacks supporting the president compared to about two-thirds of whites. For historical context, it is also useful to note that in the history of urban ethnic politics, the Barry case is not unique. In the past, newly ascendant ethnic groups (the Irish, for example) have also elected and reelected manifest scoundrels to office, apparently with the view that "yes, he is an S.O.B, but he is our S.O.B."

12. The best studies of the King case and the subsequent riots are the Gibbs study (1996), the edited volume by Gooding-Williams (1993), and Cannon's (1997) book. Cannon's book is a comprehensive job of reportage, based on interviews with nearly everyone involved—King, the officers who did the beating, the district attorney, the police chief, the prosecutors and defense lawyers in the two trials, and street cops and residents in South Central Los Angeles. The book puts reaction to the King verdict in the context of the Soon Ja Du and Latasha Harlin case. Harlin, a black teen, was shot and killed by Ja Du, a Korean merchant in South Central L.A. Although Ja Du was found guilty of manslaughter in the murder of the unarmed teen, she was given a suspended sentence and probation by the judge. This case also resulted in tensions with Koreans and protests by blacks. Finally, on the riots, see the study of television coverage by Smith (1994) and the study of local opinion dynamics after the riots by Bobo, Zubrisky, Johnson, and Oliver, 1994.

13. Perhaps the decisive decision in this case was rendered by a California State Appeals Court when it granted the defense motion for a change of venue from Los Angeles. The case was then moved to Simi Valley, a predominantly white suburb thirty-five miles from downtown Los Angeles. Home of the Ronald Reagan Presidential Library, the city has among its residents a high proportion of active and retired police officers.

14. The riots after the verdict were also in part responsible for the federal government's decision to conduct a second trial of the officers on charges of violating King's civil rights. In April 1993, two of the four officers were found guilty after a six-week trial. Although the prosecution recommended the maximum ten-year sentence under federal guidelines, the judge imposed a sentence of only thirty months. In imposing this light sentence, the judge cited several "mitigating factors," including that a second trial raised the "spectra of unfairness," that King provoked the beating, and that the officers had suffered enough.

Later, in 1994, in a civil suit against the City of Los Angeles, King was awarded $3.8 million in compensatory damages for his injuries at the hands of the police. This was much less than the $15 million sought by King, and the jury refused to award any punitive damages to King for his injuries or the violations of his civil rights.

15.   Of the many books on the Simpson case, we recommend three: First, *Race and Justice: Rodney King and O. J. Simpson in a House Divided*, a fine volume by Jewelle Taylor Gibbs (1996), the distinguished black psychologist, which examines both the Simpson and King cases in considerable factual detail and from a variety of intellectual perspectives. This volume is particularly useful in its explication of conspiracy theory as a device to analyze the cases. Second, *The Simpson Trial in Black and White*, by Elias and Schatzman (1995), because it provides perspectives from one black and one white reporter who covered the trial on a daily basis for black and white media, respectively. Last, *Madam Foreman: A Rush to Judgment?*, reflections on the case by three of the jurors (see Cooley, Bess, and Rubin-Jackson, 1995).

16.   There were also differences in opinions on bias in media coverage: 44% of blacks but only 16% of whites agreed there would have been less press coverage if Simpson had been a white celebrity, and 54% of blacks but 18% of whites agreed there would have been less press coverage if the victims had been blacks. Press coverage was indeed biased. For example, see Jacob's (1996) study, which shows that the *Los Angeles Times* tended to present the Simpson arrest and trial in an unsympathetic way, whereas the black weekly *Los Angeles Sentinel* in effect became Simpson's champion in the media, apparently reflecting the views of the city's black community as the *Los Angeles Times* reflected the views of the city's whites.

17.   Under vigorous questioning by F. Lee Bailey, another of Simpson's "dream team" attorneys, Detective Mark Fuhrman, who had found much of the incriminating evidence against Simpson, repeatedly denied ever having used the word *nigger* to refer to black people. However, it was later discovered that in taped recordings with Laura Hart McKinney, an aspiring playwright, Fuhrman had repeatedly used the word *nigger* and had also bragged about beating up blacks and Latinos, planting evidence, and other kinds of misconduct.

18.   Simpson was subsequently awarded custody by a Los Angeles family court judge. However, this judgment was overturned by a unanimous three-judge appeals court, which held that the family court judge erred by preventing introduction of evidence that Simpson may have murdered his wife. The case was sent back to the lower court for a new trial (see Marosi and Hernandez, 1998).

7

Conclusion

The United States has always been a society deeply divided by color. Surveys and polls are not available, but it is reasonable to guess that from the establishment of the Atlantic slave trade and the institutionalization of slavery as part of the American way of life, black opinion and white opinion have been profoundly divided by color, at least insofar as matters of race are concerned.[1] The differences in opinion between blacks and whites on the O. J. Simpson case and the other controversies examined in this book have their roots in the history of slavery and its psychological, cultural, economic, and political manifestations in late twentieth century America.

We began this book by noting the deep divisions in opinions between blacks and whites. These divisions are unlike any other in American society and are so widespread that scholars of race opinion routinely refer to vast gaps and gulfs between the races and suggest that these opinion differences indicate that blacks and whites live in different perceptual worlds.

Our focus and purpose in this book was to study how these divisions across the color line manifest themselves in a variety of places, times, and circumstances. But we would be remiss if we did not emphasize in this concluding chapter that although the races are divided, they are also united by a common culture and political tradition; that is, in all likelihood when all is said and done, Americans are more united by tradition and culture across the color line than they are divided.

For example, African Americans and Americans of European descent share in common the Judeo-Christian tradition, the tradition of liberal democracy and constitutionalism, the tradition of entrepreneurial capitalism, and an adherence to a common civic culture. Also, blacks and whites share a common set of beliefs

135

and values about family and community and engage in similar patterns of consumption, recreation, and leisure. These things that unite Americans across the color line are documented in opinion studies and are made manifest when Americans travel abroad. Whether white Americans in Europe or black Americans in Africa, Americans abroad come to quickly know that they are Americans—a people with distinctive ethos, outlooks, and interests.[2]

We should also emphasize in this concluding chapter that there is considerable consensus across the color line on race matters specifically. Blacks and whites are divided, but not pervasively so, on the causes and the solutions to present-day racial inequalities. Both races see multiple causes of racial inequalities in America—systemic as well as individual—while rejecting explanations that point to black inferiority. On race-specific policies, such as busing for purposes of school desegregation and affirmative action, although there are racial differences, the differences among blacks are as great as or greater than the differences between blacks and whites. And it is worth recalling the remarkable consensus on racial remedies that emerged in the polls in the aftermath of the Rodney King riots in Los Angeles.

Finally, even for most of the controversies examined in this book, not all is black or white. For example, there was no difference to speak of between blacks and whites on the Anita Hill–Clarence Thomas controversy; and a biracial consensus, however fragile and amorphous, did emerge in the aftermath of the Persian Gulf War. Blacks and whites universally viewed the verdict in the Rodney King trial as unjust. And even in the O. J. Simpson case, although there was a racial chasm on the verdict, it emerged only after a racially polarized, nationally televised trial marked by evidence of police incompetence and by rumors of police conspiracy marked by the racist lies of a leading detective in the case.

Yet we ignore the deep divisions revealed in study of these cases and controversies at society's peril. It is really quite remarkable and potentially socially dangerous that majorities or near majorities of African Americans would think it possibly or likely true that their government—a government controlled by whites—would deliberately create the plague of crack cocaine in black communities and then jail thousands and thousands of young blacks for selling and using the drug it foisted on them, that this same government would deliberately create a dangerous virus such as HIV in order to damage or destroy the black community, or that this government would seek to discredit, defame, and destroy its leaders or leaders of America that are perceived as sympathetic to blacks, such as President Kennedy.

Again, this is an extraordinary social cleavage—for a people to believe that their government would engage in a kind of slow-motion genocide. Given that large numbers of blacks believe in these racist, genocidal conspiracies, it is remarkable that support for radical black nationalist movements and leaders, such as the Nation of Islam and Louis Farrakhan, is not greater than it is among black people.

Almost as equally striking—as well as somewhat surprising—is the deep sense of alienation in large segments of the white population, for example, the almost universal belief among whites (as well as blacks) that the government itself was involved in the murder of President Kennedy and has been covering up its involvement for almost four decades. Large numbers of whites also believe that the government might be involved in drug trafficking; might be involved in a coverup of its destruction of a civilian American aircraft; or might have deliberately destroyed by fire the compound of a dissident religious sect, killing women and children. That these beliefs are unbelievable is fair enough, but that they are held by such large numbers of whites ought not be ignored.

We have endeavored to explain black opinion on conspiracism, Marion Barry, O. J. Simpson, and some of the other controversies as historically, culturally, and structurally rooted—"justified paranoia." White conspiracy opinion leaves us at a loss. Why would such large numbers of largely prosperous Americans, in a reasonably democratic polity where things are going reasonably well socially and economically, hold such paranoid views? What are the historical and structural bases for this paranoia? What does this kind of opinion among so large a segment of the white population suggest about the health of the American democracy? If these opinions are latent in an era of relative tranquility, what might happen to such opinions and how might they manifest themselves if the nation found itself in a crisis, economic, political, or racial? Would the Oklahoma City bombing and the other activities of the militant white militia become more likely? We do not know, but we believe these are issues that require much more attention from the social science community.

But our major concern in studying these cases and controversies was understanding and bridging the racial divide—the race gaps, gulfs, and chasms—rather than examining white conspiracism and alienation.

In the past decade, social scientists have developed multiple theories to account for the race divisions in opinion. Such theories include different race-group interests that separate black and white communities and class and cultural differences. Although each of these theories may have some explanatory value, we are persuaded that these gulfs and chasms in opinion are rooted in history and in the subordinate place of the black community in the nation's social structures. By *structural* we mean that as the nation enters its fourth century, black Americans are politically underrepresented, economically dispossessed, and socially and culturally stigmatized.

As we said in chapter 1 (quoting the title from the Blassingame and Berry book) blacks in the United States have a "long memory"—a long memory of the slave trade, slavery, segregation, and other forms of racial subordination and exploitation. This historical memory gives rise to a distinct culture among blacks, a culture marked by the values of freedom, moralism, resistance, and self-determination but one also marked by suspiciousness, alienation, and distrust. These historically constructed cultural memories are reinforced in the late twentieth century by what one scholar described as a "slavery unwilling to die" (Feagin, 1988)—the perception of blacks of all social classes that this historic pattern of racist subordination continues.

Given these historical, structural, and cultural sources of the racial divide, how might it be bridged? History, knowledge, and memory of it is a given that is unbridgeable. One can only seek to learn history's lessons and to avoid its errors. The history of black subjugation and its effects on black opinion is simply something that the society has to endure, a legacy that cannot be overcome.

The perceptions of continuing racism are also difficult to overcome. However, to the extent that these perceptions are rooted in present-day realities, programs and policies of racial reform and amelioration might in the long run help to bridge or to narrow the gulfs and chasms to gaps. For example, there is ample evidence of racial discrimination in the criminal justice system, from the police to the courts and prisons. Extensive, widely publicized reform in this system would ease—again in the long run—black alienation from this system that gives rise to beliefs that O. J. Simpson might have been the victim of a vast police conspiracy or that the government was out to get Marion Barry because of his effectiveness as a black leader rather than because of his misdeeds.[3] Similarly, a reconsideration of the racially discriminatory war on drugs and certainly more fairness in arrests, prosecutions, and sentencing might, again in the long run, decrease paranoia about drugs as government conspiracy. Similarly with HIV-AIDS, a more vigorous, targeted program of education and treatment should help to ameliorate black suspiciousness.

However, the key in the long run to narrowing the race divide in opinion between blacks and whites—given the burden of history—is to bridge the real-world gulfs and chasms between blacks and whites in socioeconomic well-being, political power, and status—in other words, to narrow the gap in education, housing, health, employment, income, and other indicators of race-group rank and status.

African Americans believe that in order to narrow these gaps between the races, the federal government should take an activist role with programs and policies of liberal reform in the tradition of the New Deal and the Great Society. Most whites, however, oppose such reform programs, particularly if they are targeted toward the black community and may require increases in taxes and spending. This ideological gulf is, alas, perhaps the most important of the divisions across the color line examined in this book of cases and controversies.

NOTES

1. The earliest scientific public opinion poll on race was conducted in the late 1930s by the Roper organization. It revealed a profoundly racist America. Only 13% of whites believed that blacks should be free to live wherever they wished; 50% of whites believed that whites should have the first chance at any job, and 70% said blacks were less intelligent than whites. The archives of these early polls do not report black responses. (See Morin, 1997).

2. Ninety-one percent of whites and 84% of blacks believe that the United States is a "better country than most," an insignificant difference of 7. (See *Time*, 1998.)

3. Four years following the Simpson case an internal investigation confirmed widespread corruption in the Los Angeles Police Department, along the lines suggested by Simpson's attorneys. In what is described as the largest police corruption scandal in the city's history, there were revelations of officers dealing drugs, planting guns and other evidence on innocent people, perjury, beatings, and wrongful shootings. Although more than a dozen cases have been dismissed and eleven officers suspended, the black community in Los Angeles reacted to the revelations with indifference (see Associated Press, 1999c).

Appendix

Forty-seven surveys or polls were used in this book. We identified the surveys either through the Roper Center for Public Opinion at the University of Connecticut or the Interuniversity Consortium for Political and Social Research at the University of Michigan. Some of the surveys were also acquired from these two institutions, while others were acquired directly from news organizations. We are especially grateful to the *Washington Post*, to *Southern Focus*, and to Scripps Howard/Ohio University for giving us cost-free direct access to their polls.

In this appendix, we list each of the surveys used in the book by category of controversy. We include for each survey:

1. the date of the survey
2. the sample size
3. the number of black respondents, and
4. the number of questions analyzed for use in the book.

In general, we analyzed most questions in the following manner:

Race (black or white) by question
Race by question by education (college or no college)
Race by question by gender
Race by question by age (18–29, 30–44, 45–59, 60+)

In some cases we were not always able to conduct all of the analyses just listed because in some cases the sample sizes were too small or the samples did not include education or other of the variables. In all of the surveys, except those conducted by the *Washington Post* on the Barry case, the college cohort includes those who attended some college. In Washington, because of the higher levels of education, the college cohort includes only those with college degrees.

List of Surveys

	Date	Sample Size	Number of Blacks	Number of Questions
General Social Survey (GSS)[1]	1996	2,904	402	446
American Public Opinion and U.S. Foreign Policy[2]	1994	2,605	290	160
Iraq				
Washington Post/ABC News	8/1990	769	68	25
Washington Post/ABC News	8/1990	875	85	42
Washington Post/ABC News	11/1990	810	82	20
Washington Post/ABC News	1/1991	780	78	13
Washington Post/ABC News	1/1991	544	44	8
Washington Post/ABC News	1/1991	540	44	8
Washington Post/ABC News	1/1991	531	53	15
Washington Post/ABC News	2/1991	511	43	11
Washington Post/ABC News	2/1991	520	47	15
Washington Post/ABC News	2/1991	514	37	10
Washington Post/ABC News	2/1991	778	66	14
ABC News	3/1991	1,317	137	41
Haiti				
Washington Post/ABC News	5/1994	1,523	114	6
Louis Farrakhan				
New York Times/CBS News	2/1992	1,316	291	10
Time/CNN	10/1995	1,046	500	28
Clarence Thomas/Anita Hill				
New York Times/CBS News	9/1991	1,519	324	38
New York Times/CBS News[3]	10/8, 13, 14, 1991	1,519	324	38

List of Surveys *(continued)*

	Date	Sample Size	Number of Blacks	Number of Questions
Colin Powell				
CNN/Gallup	9/1995	1,011	98	4
Conspiracies				
Drugs and AIDS[4]				
New York Times/CBS News	6/1990	1,047	136	6
New York Times/CBS News	2/1994	1,316	291	1
Southern Focus	Spring 1997	1,222	87	6
Kennedy Assassination				
CBS News	10/1993	1,117	136	6
Oklahoma Bombing				
CBS News	4/1995	596	80	9
Paranormal				
Washington Post/ABC News	5/1994	1,523	114	6
King Assassination				
CBS News	4/1998	782	NA*	1
Selected Conspiracies (FDR/Pearl Harbor, TWA Flight 800, Bombing of Branch Davidian Compound)				
Scripps Howard/Ohio University	Summer 1997	1,009	100	11
Tawana Brawley				
New York Times/CBS News	6/1998	676	280	33
Marion Barry				
Washington Post	3/1988	1,455	688	41
Washington Post	1/1990	661	404	8
Washington Post	2/1990	1,264	708	8
Washington Post	2/1990	1,354	777	21
Washington Post	8/1990	597	404	17
Washington Post	12/1993	994	542	58
Washington Post	9/1994	1,538	766	41
Washington Post	January–February 1995	804	409	45
Washington Post	5/1996	806	394	32
Washington Post	2/1996	267	147	54
Washington Post	April–May 1997	1,004	535	51
Harvard University	March–April 1998	248	138	15

List of Surveys *(continued)*

	Date	Sample Size	Number of Blacks	Number of Questions
Rodney King				
New York Times	5/1992	1,254	318	46
Washington Post/ABC News	5/1992	1,144	200	17
Washington Post/ABC News	4/1992	606	154	12
O. J. Simpson				
New York Times/CBS News	6/1994	586	71	7
New York Times/CBS News	7/1994	601	66	9
New York Times/CBS News	7/1994	1,306	166	13
CBS News	September–October 1995	1,569	304	21
Washington Post	10/1995	684	312	25
Newsweek	2/1997	786	266	10

NOTES

*Not Available.

1. National Opinion Research Center, University of Chicago.

2. The Gallup organization conducted this poll for the Chicago Council on Foreign Relations.

3. This was a panel survey (the same people were interviewed at three different points in time).

4. The *New York Times*/CBS News poll was conducted only in New York City.

References

Allen, R., M. Dawson, and R. Brown. 1989. "A Schema-Based Approach to Modeling An African American Belief System." *American Political Science Review* 83: 421–41.

Associated Press. 1999a. "Clinton Foreign Policy Ranked No. 1." *New York Times on the Web*. March 15.

———. 1999b. "Civil Rights Cases Rarely Tried." *New York Times on the Web*. March 20.

———. 1999c. "LAPD Scandal Not Sparking Outrage." *New York Times on the Web*. December 12.

Barras, J. 1998. *The Last of the Black Emperors: The Hollow Comeback of Marion Barry in the New Age of Black Leaders*. New York: Bancroft Press.

Bell, D. 1980. *Race, Racism and American Law*. Boston: Little, Brown.

Bennett, L. 1967. *Before the Mayflower*. Baltimore: Penguin Books.

Bennett, W., and D. Paletz. 1994. *Taken by Storm: The Media, Public Opinion, and U.S. Foreign Policy in the Gulf War*. Chicago: University of Chicago Press.

Berry, M., and J. Blassingame. 1982. *Long Memory: The Black Experience in America*. New York: Oxford University Press.

Biskupic, J. 1995. "Has the Court Lost Its Appeal?" *Washington Post*. October 12.

Bobo, L., J. Klugel, and R. Smith. 1997. "Laissez Faire Racism: The Crystallization of a Kinder Gentler Anti-Black Ideology." In *Racial Attitudes in the 1980s: Continuity and Change*, edited by S. Tuch and J Martin. Westport, CT: Praeger.

Bobo, L., C. Zubrisky, J. Johnson, and M. Oliver. 1994. "Public Opinion before and after a Spring of Discontent." In *The Los Angeles Riots: Lessons for the Urban Future*, edited by M. Baldassare. Boulder: Westview Press.

Breed, A. 1999. "Party Has Succession in Store for the South." *West County Times*. June 20.

Breitman, G. 1966. *Malcolm X Speaks.* New York: Grove Press.

Brink, W., and L. Harris. 1964. *The Negro Revolution in America.* New York: Simon and Schuster.

———. *Black and White: A Study of U.S. Racial Attitudes.* New York: Simon & Schuster.

Brock, D. 1993. *The Real Anita Hill: The Untold Story.* New York: Free Press.

Bronner, E. 1983. *Battle for Justice: How the Bork Nomination Shook America.* New York: Norton.

Brooks, J. 1995. "Court Allows Denver to End 21-Year Busing Experiment and Return to Neighborhood Schools." *New York Times,* September 17.

Brown, R., and M. Wolford. 1994. "Religious Resources and African American Political Action." *National Political Science Review* 4: 30–48.

Bureau of Labor Statistics. 1999. "The Employment Situation." Press Release, U.S. Department of Labor, Washington, DC. April.

Button, J. 1978. *Black Violence: Political Impact of the 1960s Riots.* Princeton: Princeton University Press.

Cannon, Lou. 1997. *Official Negligence: How Rodney King and the Riots Changed Los Angeles and the LAPD.* New York: Times Books.

Carlson, T. 1996. "A Disgraceful Newspaper Expose and Its Fans." *The Weekly Standard,* September 30.

Carmen, J. 1996. "TV in Black and White." *San Francisco Chronicle,* August 26, sec. E, p. 1.

Case, C. 1998. *The Slaughter: An American Atrocity.* Asheville, NC: Rusty Denham/First Biltmore.

Chirimula, R., and R. Chirimula. 1987. *AIDS, Africa, and Racism.* North Derby on Trent, U.K.: Richard Chirimula.

Clay, G. 1997. "A Black Journalist Urges O. J. To Admit Truth." *New York Times,* February 9.

Clegg, C. 1997. *An Original Man: The Life and Times of Elijah Muhammad.* New York: St. Martin's Press.

Cline, F. 1993. "Campaign Is a Fraud to the Urban Underclass." *New York Times,* October 3.

Cochran, D. 1999. *The Color of Liberalism: Race and Contemporary American Liberalism.* Albany: SUNY Press.

Cole, D. 1999. *No Equal Justice: Race and Class in the American Criminal Justice System.* New York: The Free Press.

Cooley, A., A. Bess, and M. Rubin-Jackson. 1995. *Madam Foreman: A Rush to Judgment?* Beverly Hills, CA: Cove Books.

Condran, J. 1979. "Changes in White Attitudes toward Blacks, 1963–67." *Public Opinion Quarterly* 43: 463–76.

Conti, J., and B. Stetson. 1989. *Challenging the Civil Rights Establishment: Profiles of a New Black Vanguard*. Westport, CT: Praeger.

Converse, P. 1964. "The Nature of Belief Systems in Mass Public." In *Ideology and Its Discontent*, edited by D. Apter. New York: Free Press.

Cox, O. 1959. *Caste, Class, and Race: A Study in Social Dynamics*. New York: Monthly Review.

Cruse, H. 1987. *Plural but Equal: Blacks and Minorities in America*. New York: Morrow.

Curry, G., ed. 1996. *The Affirmative Action Debate*. Reading, MA: Addison-Wesley.

Curry, R. 1972. *Conspiracy: The Fear of Subversion in American History*. (Austin, TX: Holt, Rinehart and Winston.

Davis, M. 1990. *City of Quartz: Excavating the Future in Los Angeles*. New York: Verso Press.

Davis, S. 1995. "Affirmative Action: The Quality of the Debate." *National Political Science Review* 5: 263–69.

Dawson, M. 1994. *Behind the Mule: Race and Class in African American Politics*. Princeton, NJ: Princeton University Press.

———. 1995. "Structure and Ideology: The Shaping of Black Public Opinion." Paper prepared for presentation at the 1995 Annual Meeting of the Midwest Political Science Association.

Dawson, M., and R. Brown. 1995. "Black Discontent: The Preliminary Report of the 1993–94 National Black Politics Study" Report #1. University of Chicago.

Dawson, R. 1967. *American Negro Folklore*. New York: Fawcett.

Deconde, A. 1992. *Ethnicity, Race, and American Foreign Policy: A History*. Boston: Northeastern University Press.

Dewey, J. 1927. *The Public and Its Problems*. New York: Henry Holt.

Dorman, W., and S. Livingston. 1994. "The Establishing Phase of the Persian Gulf War." In *Taken by Storm: The Media, Public Opinion, and U.S. Foreign Policy in the Gulf War*, edited by W. Bennett and D. Paletz. Chicago: University of Chicago Press.

Douglass, F. [1892] 1968. *Narrative of the Life of Frederick Douglass*. New York: Signet.

Dryer, R. 1999. *White*. New York: Routledge.

Duke, L. 1991. "Emerging Black Anti-War Movement Rooted in Domestic Issues." *Washington Post*, February 8.

Elias, T., and D. Schatzman. 1995. *The Simpson Trial in Black and White*. Los Angeles: Ten Speed Press.

Entman, R., and B. Page. 1994. "The News before the Storm: The Iraq War Debate and the Limits to Media Independence." In *Taken by Storm: The Media, Public Opinion, and U.S. Foreign Policy in the Gulf War*, edited by W. Bennett and D. Paletz. Chicago: University of Chicago Press.

Epstein, E. 1966. *Inquest: The Warren Commission and the Establishment of Truth.* New York: Viking.

Erskine, H. 1973. "The Polls: Race Relations." *Public Opinion Quarterly* 26: 132–47.

Feagin, J. 1988. "A Slavery Unwilling to Die." *Journal of Black Studies* 18: 451–69.

Fierce, M. 1982. "Black and White Opinions toward South Africa." *Journal of Modern African Studies* 20: 669–87.

Final Call. 1996. "The CIA Drug Lords." September 3: 16.

Flax, J. 1998. *The American Dream in Black and White: The Clarence Thomas Hearings.* Ithaca, NY: Cornell University Press.

Frady, M. 1996. *Jesse: The Life and Pilgrimage of Jesse Jackson.* New York: Random House.

Frank, L. 1995. "U.S. Courts Give Blacks Longer Terms." *West County Times,* September 24. (Reprinted from the *Nashville Tennessean.*)

Franklin, J. H. [1947] 1967. *From Slavery to Freedom.* New York: Knopf.

Franklin, V. P. 1984. *Black Self-Determination.* Westport, CT: Lawrence Hill.

Fullwood, S. 1993. "Congressional Black Caucus Turns Up Heat on Clinton." *Los Angeles Times,* June 11.

Gardell, M. 1996. *In the Name of Elijah Muhammad: Louis Farrakhan and the Nation of Islam.* Durham, NC: Duke University Press.

Garrow, D. 1981. *The FBI and Martin Luther King, Jr.* New York: Penguin.

Gates, H. 1995. "Powell and the Black Elite." *New Yorker,* September 25.

Gearan, A. 1999. "U.S. Prison Population Has Doubled Since 1985." *West County Times,* March 15.

Genovese, E. 1974. *Roll Jordan Roll: The World the Slaves Made.* New York: Pantheon.

George, N. 1989. *The Death of Rhythm and Blues.* New York: Pantheon.

Gibbs, J. T. 1996. *Race and Justice: Rodney King and O. J. Simpson in a House Divided.* San Francisco: Jossey-Bass.

Goldberg, J. 1999. "The Color of Suspicion." *New York Times Magazine,* June 20.

Golden, T. 1996. "Tale of CIA and Drugs Has Life of Its Own." *New York Times,* October 21.

Gooding-Williams, R. 1993. *Reading Rodney King/Reading Urban Uprising.* Boulder, CO:Westview.

Gordon, E., and D. Rollock. 1987. Commincentric Frames of Reference in Pursuit of Knowledge. Unpublished manuscript, Program in Afro-American Studies, Yale University.

Graham, H. 1990. *The Civil Rights Era.* New York: Oxford University Press.

Gregory, S. 1998. *Black Corona: Race and the Politics of Place in an Urban Community.* Princeton, NJ: Princeton University Press.

Gurin, P., S. Hatchett, and J. Jackson. 1989. *Hope and Independence: Blacks' Response to Electoral and Party Politics.* New York: Russell Sage Foundation.

Hacker, A. 1992. *Two Nations: Black, White, Separate, Hostile, Unequal.* New York: Scribners.

Hagner, P., and J. Pierce. 1984. "Racial Differences and Political Conceptualization." *Western Political Quarterly* 37: 212–35.

Hall, K., W. Wiecek, and P. Finkelman. 1991. *American Legal History: Cases and Materials.* New York, Oxford University Press.

Hallin, D., and T. Gitlin. 1994. "The Gulf War As Popular Culture and Television Drama." In *Taken by Storm: The Media, Public Opinion, and U.S. Foreign Policy in the Gulf War,* edited by W. Bennett and D. Paletz. Chicago: University of Chicago Press.

Hampton, B. 1967. "On Identification and Negro Tricksters." *Southern Folklore Quarterly* 31: 55–65.

Harding, V. 1981. *There Is a River: The Black Struggle for Freedom in America.* Orlando, FL: Harcourt Brace Jovanovich.

Harris, C. 1995. *Congress and the Governance of the Nation's Capital.* Washington, DC: Georgetown University Press.

Harris, D. 1999. *The Logic of Black Urban Rebellions: Challenging the Dynamics of White Domination in Miami.* Westport, CT: Praeger.

Harris, F. 1994. "Something Within: Religion As a Mobilizer of African American Political Activism." *Journal of Politics* 56: 48–65.

Harris, L. 1978. *A Study of Attitudes toward Racial and Religious Minorities and Women.* New York: National Conference of Christians and Jews.

Harris, R. 1990. "Blacks Feel Brunt of Drug War." *Los Angeles Times,* April 22.

Henderson, E. 1995. *Afrocentrism and World Politics: Toward a New Paradigm.* Westport, CT: Praeger.

Hennessy, B. 1985. *Public Opinion.* New York: Brooks/Cole.

Henry, C. 1990. *Culture and African American Politics.* Bloomington: Indiana University Press.

Henry, W. 1994. "Pride and Prejudice." *Time,* February 28.

Hernstein, R., and C. Murray. 1994. *The Bell Curve: Intelligence and Class Structure in America.* New York: Free Press.

Hill, A. 1997. *Speaking Truth to Power.* New York: Doubleday.

Hill, M. 1998. "Jury Rules Three Men Defamed Prosecutor." *West County Times,* June 14.

Hirschberg, L. 1994. "The White World of O. J. Simpson." *New York,* August 29.

Hochschild, J. 1995. *Facing Up to the American Dream: Race, Class, and the Soul of a Nation.* Princeton, NJ: Princeton University Press.

Hofstader, R. 1979. *The Paranoid Style in American Politics.* Chicago: University of Chicago Press.

Holden, M. 1973. *The Politics of the Black "Nation."* New York: Chandler.

Holmes, M., D. Hodges, and J. Rich. 1989. "Letter to the Editor." *Journal of the American Medical Association* 261 (June).

Holmes, S. 1994. "With Persuasion and Muscle Black Caucus Reshapes Haiti Policy." *New York Times*, July 7.

Hoy, R. 1992. "Lid on a Boiling Pot." In *The New Right Papers*, edited by R. Whitaker. New York: St. Martin's.

Huggins, N. 1971. "Afro-American History: Myths, Heroes, and Reality." In *Key Issues in the Afro-American Experience*, edited by M. Kilson, D. Fox, and N. Huggins. New York: Harcourt Brace Jovanovich.

Hulbert, J. 1989. "The Southern Region: A Test of the Hypothesis of Cultural Distinctiveness." *The Sociological Quarterly* 30: 245–66.

Ignatiev, N. 1995. *How the Irish Became White*. (New York: Routledge.

Ignatiev, N., and J. Garvey, eds. 1996. *Race Traitor*. New York: Routledge.

Irvine, M. 1999. "Illegal Gun Dealer Sold Weapon to Racist." *West County Times*, July 7.

Jackson, R. 1998. "Traffic Stop Measure Appears to Be Doomed." *West County Times*, June 2.

Jacobs, R. 1996. "Civil Society and Crisis: Culture, Discourse, and the Rodney King Beating." *American Journal of Sociology* 101: 1238–72.

Jaffe, H., and T. Sherwood. 1994. *Dream City: Race, Power, and the Decline of Washington, D.C.* New York: Simon & Schuster.

Jaynes, G., and R. Williams. 1989. *A Common Destiny: Blacks and American Society*. Washington, DC: National Academy Press.

Jet. 1995. "Million Man March Draws More Than 1 Million Black Men to Washington." October 30.

Jet. 1999a. "Gap between Black and White Viewing Narrows." May 17.

Jet. 1999b. "Memphis Jury Decides Rev. Martin Luther King Jr. Was Victim of Conspiracy." December 27.

Johnson, G. 1983. *Architects of Fear: Conspiracy Theories and Paranoia in American Politics*. Los Angeles: J. P. Tarcher.

Jones, J. 1982. *Bad Blood, the Tuskegee Syphilis Experiment: Tragedy of Race and Medicine*. New York: Free Press.

Jones, M. 1999. "Affirmative Action: What Is the Question—Race or Oppression." *National Political Science Review* 7: 248–49.

Jones, R. 1990. "The Myth of Afro-American Communalism: Elements of a Black Psychology." Unpublished manuscript, Brown University.

Kalb, M. 1994. "A View from the Press." In *Taken by Storm: The Media, Public Opinion, and U.S. Foreign Policy in the Gulf War*, edited by W. Bennett and D. Paletz. Chicago: University of Chicago Press.

Katner, P., and G. Pankey. 1989. "Evidence for a Euro-American Origin Human Immunodeficiency Virus." *Journal of American Medical Association* 79: 1068–72.

Katz, J. 1996. "Tracking the Genesis of the Crack Trade." *Los Angeles Times*, October 20.

Katznelson, I. 1971. "Power in the Reformulation of Race Relations Research." In *Race,*

Change, and Urban Society, edited by W. Ellis and P. Orleans. Newbury Park, CA: Sage.

Keil, C. 1966. *Urban Blues*. Chicago: University of Chicago Press.

Kennedy, R. 1988. "*McClesky v. Kemp*: Race, Capital Punishment, and the Supreme Court." *Harvard Law Review* 101.

———. 1997. *Race, Crime, and Law*. New York: Pantheon.

Key, V. O. 1961. *Public Opinion and American Democracy*. New York: Knopf.

Kilson, M. 1964. "Toward Freedom: An Analysis of Slave Revolts in the United States." *Phylon* 25: 175–87.

Kinder, D. 1983. "Diversity and Complexity in American Public Opinion." In *The State of the Discipline*, edited by A. Finifter. Washington, DC: American Political Science Association.

Kinder, D., and L. Sanders. 1996. *Divided by Color: Racial Politics and Democratic Ideals*. Chicago: University of Chicago Press.

Knowles, L., and K. Prewitt. 1969. *Institutional Racism in America*. Upper Saddle River, NJ: Prentice-Hall.

Krenn, M. 1998. *Black Diplomacy: African Americans in the State Department*. Armonk, NY: M. E. Sharpe.

Kroeber, A., and C. Kluckhorn. 1952. *Culture: A Critical Review of Concepts and Definitions*. New York: Peabody Museum of Archaeology and Ethnology.

Lane, M. 1966. *Rush to Judgment: A Critique of the Warren Commission Inquiry into the Murder of President John F. Kennedy, Officer J. D. Tippitt, and Lee Harvey Oswald*. (Austin, TX: Holt, Rinehart and Winston.

Lane, R., and D. Sears. 1964. *Public Opinion*. Upper Saddle River, NJ: Prentice-Hall.

Lee, M., and B. Shlain. *Acid Dreams? The Complete History of LSD, the CIA, the Sixties, and Beyond*. New York: Grove Widenfeld.

Leonard, J. 1984. "Employment and Occupational Advance under Affirmative Action." *Review of Economics and Statistics* 66: 377–85.

Lersch, K. 1993. Current Trends in Police Brutality: An Analysis of Recent Newspaper Accounts. Master's thesis, University of Florida.

Lester, W. 1999. "Many Think Police Have Racial Bias." *West County Times*, December 11.

Lincoln, C. 1961. *The Black Muslims in America*. Boston: Beacon.

Lincoln, C., and L. Mamiya. 1990. *The Black Church in America*. Durham, NC: Duke University Press.

Lippman, W. 1922. *Public Opinion*. New York: Penguin.

Lipset, S., and E. Raab. 1978. *The Politics of Unreason: Right Wing Extremism in America*. Chicago: University of Chicago Press.

Loury, G. 1985. "The Moral Quandary of the Black Community." *The Public Interest* 15: 11–17.

Lumumba, C., I. Obdele, and N. Taifa. 1995. *Reparations Now!* (Baton Rouge, LA: The House of Songhay.

Lusanne, C., and J. Steele. 1994. "A Fatal Attraction: The Firing of Ben Chavis by the NAACP." *Black Political Agenda* 2: 1, 10–13.

Madhubuti, H., and R. Karenga. 1996. *Million Man March/Day of Absence: A Commemorative.* Chicago: Third World Press.

Magida, A. 1996. *Prophet of Rage: A Life of Louis Farrakhan and His Nation.* New York: Basic Books.

Mamiya, L. 1982. "From Black Muslim to Bialian: The Evolution of a Movement." *Journal for the Scientific Study of Religion* 21.

Marosi, R., and G. Hernandez. 1998. "Simpson Custody Ruling Overturned." *West County Times,* November 11.

Marx, G. 1967. *Protest and Prejudice: A Study of Belief in Black America.* New York: Harper and Row.

Massey, D., and N. Denton. 1990. "American Apartheid: Segregation and the Making of the Underclass." *American Journal of Sociology* 96: 329–57.

———. 1988. "Suburbanization and Segregation in U.S. Metropolitan Areas." *American Journal of Sociology* 94: 592–626.

Matthews, D., and J. Protho. 1966. *Negroes and the New Southern Politics.* New York: Harcourt Brace.

Mauer, M. 1995. *Young Black Men and the Criminal Justice System.* Washington, DC: The Sentencing Project.

Mayer, J., and J. Abramson. 1994. *Strange Justice: The Clarence Thomas–Anita Hill Story.* Boston: Houghton Mifflin.

McBride, D. 1991. *From TB to AIDS: Epidemics among Urban Blacks Since 1900.* Albany: SUNY Press.

McCormick, J. 1997. "The Message and the Messengers: Opinions from the Million Man March." *National Political Science Review* 6: 142–64.

McCoy, A. 1991. *The Politics of Heroin: CIA Complicity in the Drug Trade.* New York: Lawrence.

McKee, J. 1993. *Sociology and the Race Problem: The Failure of a Perspective.* Urbana, IL: University of Illinois Press.

Miller, J. 1978. *The Black Presence in American Foreign Policy.* Washington, DC: Howard University Press.

Mills, N. (ed). 1973. *The Great School Bus Controversy.* New York: Teachers College Press.

Mollenkopf, J. 1990. "New York: The Great Anomaly." In *Racial Politics in American Cities,* edited by R. Browning, D. Marshall, and D. Tabb. New York: Longman.

Morin, R. 1997. "The Ugly Way We Were." *Washington Post,* April 6.

Morley, M., and C. McGillion. 1997. "'Disobedient' Generals and the Politics of

Redemocratization: The Clinton Administration and Haiti." *Political Science Quarterly* 112: 363–84.

Morrison, T. 1992. *Racing Justice, En-gendering Power: Essays on Anita Hill, Clarence Thomas, and the Construction of Social Reality.* New York: Pantheon.

Mueller, C. 1988. "The Empowerment of Women: Polling and the Women's Voting Bloc." In *The Politics of the Gender Gap: The Social Construction of Influence,* edited by C. Mueller. Newbury Park, CA: Sage.

Mueller, J. 1973. *War, Presidents, and Public Opinion.* New York: Wiley.

Mydans, S. 1991. "Officers in LA Joked about Beating Blacks." *New York Times,* March 19.

Myrdal, G. [1944] 1962. *An American Dilemma: The Negro Problem and Modern Democracy.* New York: Harper and Row.

New York Times. 1996. "Justice System Holds about 3% of U.S. Population." July 2.

Nie, N., S. Verba, and J. Petrocik. 1976. *The Changing American Voter.* Cambridge, MA: Harvard University Press.

Ogletree, C. 1995. "Blind Justice?: Race, The Constitution, and the Justice System." In *African Americans and the Constitution,* edited by J. Franklin and G. McNeil. Washington, DC: Smithsonian Institution.

Oliver, M., and T. Shapiro. 1995. *Black Wealth/White Wealth: A New Perspective on Racial Equality.* New York: Routledge.

O'Reilly, K. 1994. *Racial Matters: The FBI's Secret File on Black America, 1960–72.* New York: Carroll & Graf.

Orfield, G. 1996. *Dismantling Desegregation: The Quiet Reversal of Brown v. Board of Education.* New York: Norton.

Palmer, R. 1981. *Deep Blues.* New York: Viking.

Payne, L. 1989. "Tawayna Made It Up." *Newsday,* April 27.

Persons, G., and L. Henderson. 1990. "Mayor of the Colony: Effective Mayoral Leadership as a Matter of Public Perception." *National Political Science Review* 2: 145–53.

Phelps, T., and H. Winternitz. 1992. *Capital Games: Clarence Thomas, Anita Hill, and the Story of a Supreme Court Nomination.* New York: Hyperion.

Pipes, D. 1997. *Conspiracy.* New York: Free Press.

Poinsett, A. 1973. "Class Patterns in Black Politics." *Ebony,* August.

Powell, C. 1995. *My American Journey.* New York: Random House.

Reed, A. 1995. "Demobilization in the New Black Political Regime: Ideological Capitulation in the Post-Segregation Era." In *The Bubbling Cauldron: Race, Ethnicity, and Urban Crisis,* edited by M. Smith and J. Feagin. Minneapolis: University of Minnesota Press.

Reed, J. 1983. *Southerners: An Essay on the Social Psychology of Sectionalism.* Chapel Hill: University of North Carolina Press.

Reese, L., and R. Brown. 1995. "The Effects of Religious Messages on Racial Identity and System Blame among Blacks on African Americans." *Journal of Politics* 57: 24–39.

Reynolds, B. 1996. "White Power Brokers Ignore CIA-Drug Issue." *USA Today*, April 3.

Rich, S. 1974. "Bus Ban Defeated 47 to 48." *Washington Post*. May 16.

Rokeach, M. 1968. *Beliefs, Attitudes, and Values*. San Francisco: Jossey- Bass.

Rothstein, E. 1999. "In a Word, Culture Means Anything, Bad as Well as Good." *New York Times on the Web*, June 12.

Rousseau, J. [1762] 1955. *The Social Contract*. Chicago: Henry Regrey.

Salins, P. 1996. *Assimilation American Style*. New York: Basic.

Sawyer, M. 1977. *The Dilemma of Black Politics: A Report on Harassment of Black Elected Official*.A report prepared for the National Association of Human Rights Workers.

Scott, P., and J. Marshall. 1991. *Cocaine Politics: Drugs, Armies, and the CIA in Central America*. Berkeley: University of California Press.

Schuman, H., C. Steeth, and L. Bobo. 1985. *Racial Attitudes in America: Trends and Interpretations*. Cambridge, MA: Harvard University Press.

Sears, D. 1988. "Symbolic Racism." In *Eliminating Racism*, edited by P. Katz and D. Taylor. New York: Plenum.

Sears, D., J. Citrin, and C. Van Laar. 1995. "Black Exceptionalism in Multicultural Society." Paper prepared for presentation at the 1995 Annual Meeting of the American Political Science Association.

Sears, D., C. Hensler, and L. Speer. 1979. "White Opposition to Busing: Self-Interest or Symbolic Politics." *American Political Science Review* 73: 369–84.

Seltzer, R., J. Newman, and M. Leighton. 1997. *Sex As a Political Variable: Women As Candidates and Women As Voters in U.S. Elections*. Boulder, CO: Lynne Rienner.

Seltzer, R., and R. Smith. 1988. "Racial Differences and Intraracial Differences among Blacks in Attitudes toward AIDS." *AIDS and Public Policy Journal* 3(Fall): 31–35.

———. 1991. "Color Differences in the Afro-American Community and the Differences They Make." *Journal of Black Studies* 21: 279–86.

Sigelman, L., and S. Welch. 1994. *Black Americans' Views of Inequality: The Dream Deferred*. Cambridge, MA: Cambridge University Press.

Sims, M. (ed.). 1995. *Economic Perspectives on Affirmative Action*. Lanham, MD: University Press of America.

Singh, R. 1997. *Louis Farrakhan: Race, Reaction, and the Paranoid Style in American Politics*. Washington, DC: Georgetown University Press.

Skinner, E. 1992. *African Americans and U.S. Foreign Policy, 1850–1924*. Vol. 1. Washington, DC: Howard University Press.

Smith, E. 1994. "Transmitting Race: The Los Angeles Riots in Television News." Research paper #R-H, Joan Shorenstein Barone Center, Harvard University, John F. Kennedy School of Government.

Smith, R. 1988. "Sources of Urban Ethnic Politics: A Comparison of Alternative Explanations." In *Research on Race and Ethnic Relations*, Vol. 5, edited by C. Marrett and C. Leggon. Greenwich, CT: JAI Press.

———. (1990a). "Recent Elections and Black Politics: The Maturation or Death of Black Politics?" *PS* 22(June): 160–62.

———. (1990b). "Black Leaders Silence on Barry a Mistake." *San Francisco Chronicle*, August 1.

———. 1992. "Ideology as the Enduring Dilemma of Black Politics." In *Dilemmas of Black Politics*, edited by G. Persons. New York: HarperCollins.

———. 1995. *Racism in the Post–Civil Rights Era: Now You See It, Now You Don't.* Albany: SUNY Press.

———. 1996. *We Have No Leaders: African Americans in the Post–Civil Rights Era.* Albany: SUNY Press.

Smith, R., and R. Seltzer. 1992. *Race, Class, and Culture: A Study in Afro-American Mass Opinion.* Albany: SUNY Press.

Smith, R., and H. Walton. 1994. "U-Turn: Martin Kilson and Black Conservatism." *Transition* 62: 209–16.

Sniderman, P. 1993. "The New Look in Public Opinion Research." In *The State of the Discipline*, edited by A. Finifter. Washington, DC: American Political Science Association.

Sniderman, P., and M. Hagan. 1985. *Race and Inequality: A Study in American Values.* Chatham, NJ: Chatham House.

Sniderman, P., T. Piazza, P. Tetock, and A. Kendrick. 1991. "The New Racism." *American Journal of Political Science* 35: 423–47.

Spier, H. 1950. "Historical Developments of Public Opinion." *American Journal of Sociology* 55: 355–78.

Stanford, Karin. 1997. *Beyond the Boundaries: Rev. Jesse Jackson in International Affairs.* Albany: SUNY Press.

Steeth, C., and M. Krysan. 1996. "Affirmative Action and the Public, 1970–1995." *Public Opinion Quarterly* 60: 128–58.

Stolberg, S. 1998. "AIDS Is Epidemic among Blacks." *West County Times*, June 29.

Stuckey, S. 1987. *Slave Culture: Foundations of Nationalist Theory.* New York: Oxford University Press.

Suro, R., and M. Fletcher. 1999. "Mississippi Massacre, or Myth: Army Tries to Put to Rest Allegations of 1943 Slaughter of Black Troops." *Washington Post*, December 23.

Suro, R. and W. Pincus. 1996. "The CIA–Crack Connection: Evidence Is Lacking of Contra-Tied Plot." *Washington Post*, October 4.

Taibi, M., and H. Sims-Phillips. 1989. *Unholy Alliances: Working the Tawana Brawley Story.* New York: Harcourt Brace Jovanovich.

Tate, K., et.al. 1988. *The 1984 National Black Election Study Sourcebook.* Ann Arbor: University of Michigan, Program for Research on Black Americans, Institute for Social Research.

References

Tate, K. 1994. *From Protest to Politics: The New Black Voters in American Elections.* Cambridge, MA: Harvard University Press.

Thernstrom, A., and S. Thernstrom. 1998. *America in Black and White: One Nation, Indivisible.* New York: Simon & Schuster.

Time. 1996. "*Time's* 25 Most Influential People." June 17.

Time. 1998. November 30:35.

Tompkins, S. 1993. "Army Feared King, Secretly Watched Him, Spying on Blacks Started 75 Years Ago." *Memphis Commercial Appeal,* March 21.

Transition. 1999. "The White Issue." Vol. 73.

Trento, S. 1992. *The Power House.* New York: St. Martin's.

Turner, P. 1993. *I Heard It through the Grapevine: Rumor in African American Culture.* Berkeley: University of California Press.

U.S. Bureau of the Census. n.d. *The Social and Economic Status of the Black Population in the United States: An Historical View 1790–1978.* Washington, DC: Government Printing Office.

———. 1995. *The Black Population in the United States, March 1994 and 1993.* Washington, DC: Government Printing Office.

U.S. National Advisory Commission on Civil Disorders, Report. 1968. New York: Putnam.

Van der Berghe, P. 1967. *Race and Racism.* New York: Wiley.

Walters, R. 1987. "White Racial Nationalism in the United States. Washington, DC: Eaford.

———. 1992. "Two Political Traditions: Black Politics in the 1990s." *National Political Science Review* 3: 198–208.

———. 1995. "Colin Powell: Patriot, Icon, Enigma." *San Francisco Chronicle,* July 21.

———. 1999. *White Nationalism in the Second Reconstruction.* Manuscript, University of Maryland.

———. 1991. "Thomas Estranged from His Blackness." *Washington Post,* July 16.

Walters, R., and R. Smith. 1999. *African American Leadership.* Albany: SUNY Press.

Walton, H. 1985. *Invisible Politics: Black Political Behavior.* Albany: SUNY Press.

———. 1997. *African American Power and Politics: The Political Context Variable.* New York: Columbia University Press.

Walton, H., and R. Smith. 2000. *American Politics and the African American Quest for Universal Freedom.* New York: Addison, Wesley, Longman.

Warren, D. 1976. *The Radical Center.* South Bend, IN: Notre Dame University Press.

Webb, G. 1996. "Dark Alliance: The Story behind the Crack Explosion." *San Jose Mercury News,* August 18–20.

———. 1998. *Dark Alliances: The CIA, the Contras, and the Crack Cocaine Explosion.* New York: Seven Stories Press.

Wiener, T. 1998. "As Expected, CIA Denies Drug-Contra Link." *New York Times,* January 30.

Wienstein, B., and A. Segal. 1992. *Haiti: The Failure of Politics*. New York: Praeger.

Williams, J. 1987. "The Imperial Mayor." *The New Republic*. October 26, 21–23.

———. 1994. "President Colin Powell?" *Reconstruction* 2: 67–78.

Wood, T., and S. Stolberg. 1991. "Patrol Car Log in Beating Released." *Los Angeles Times*, March 19.

Woodward, B. 1991. *The Commanders*. New York: Simon & Schuster.

Wright, S. 1995. *Armageddon at Waco: Critical Perspectives on the Branch Davidian Conflict*. Chicago: University of Chicago Press.

Yette, S. 1998. "Dr. King's Death: An Inside Job." *Richmond (Virginia) Free Press*, April 2–4.

Zaller, J. 1994. "Elite Leadership of Mass Opinion: New Evidence from the Gulf War." In *Taken by Storm: The Media, Public Opinion, and U.S. Foreign Policy and the Persian Gulf War*, edited by L. Bennett and D. Paletz. Chicago: University of Chicago Press.

Zoglin, R. 1997. "Not So Hot Copy." *Newsweek*, May 26.

Index

About the Authors

Robert C. Smith is Professor of Political Science at San Francisco State University. Richard Seltzer is Professor of Political Science at Howard University. Together they have authored numerous papers and articles on race opinion, as well as *Race, Class, and Culture: A Study in Afro-American Mass Opinion.*